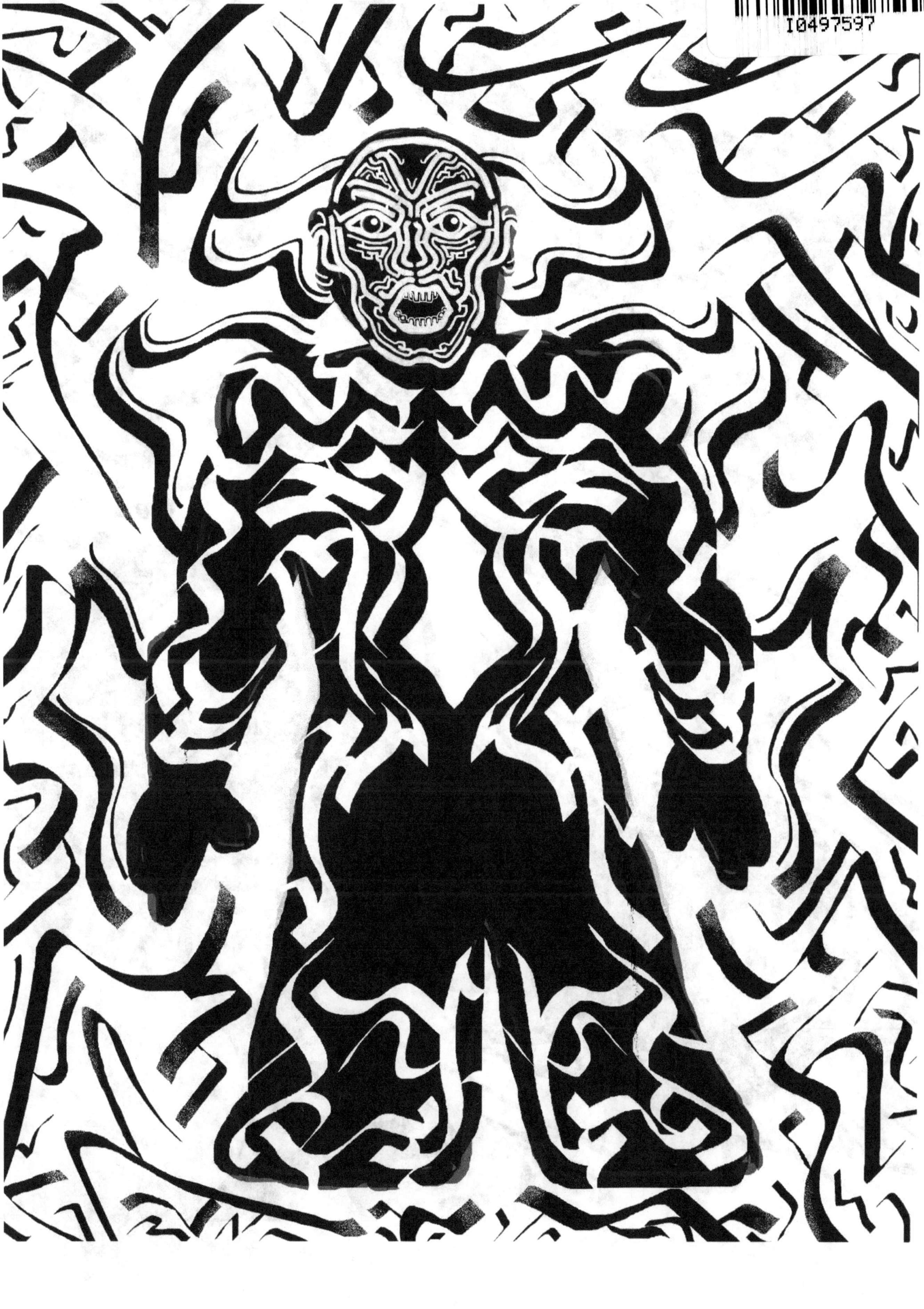

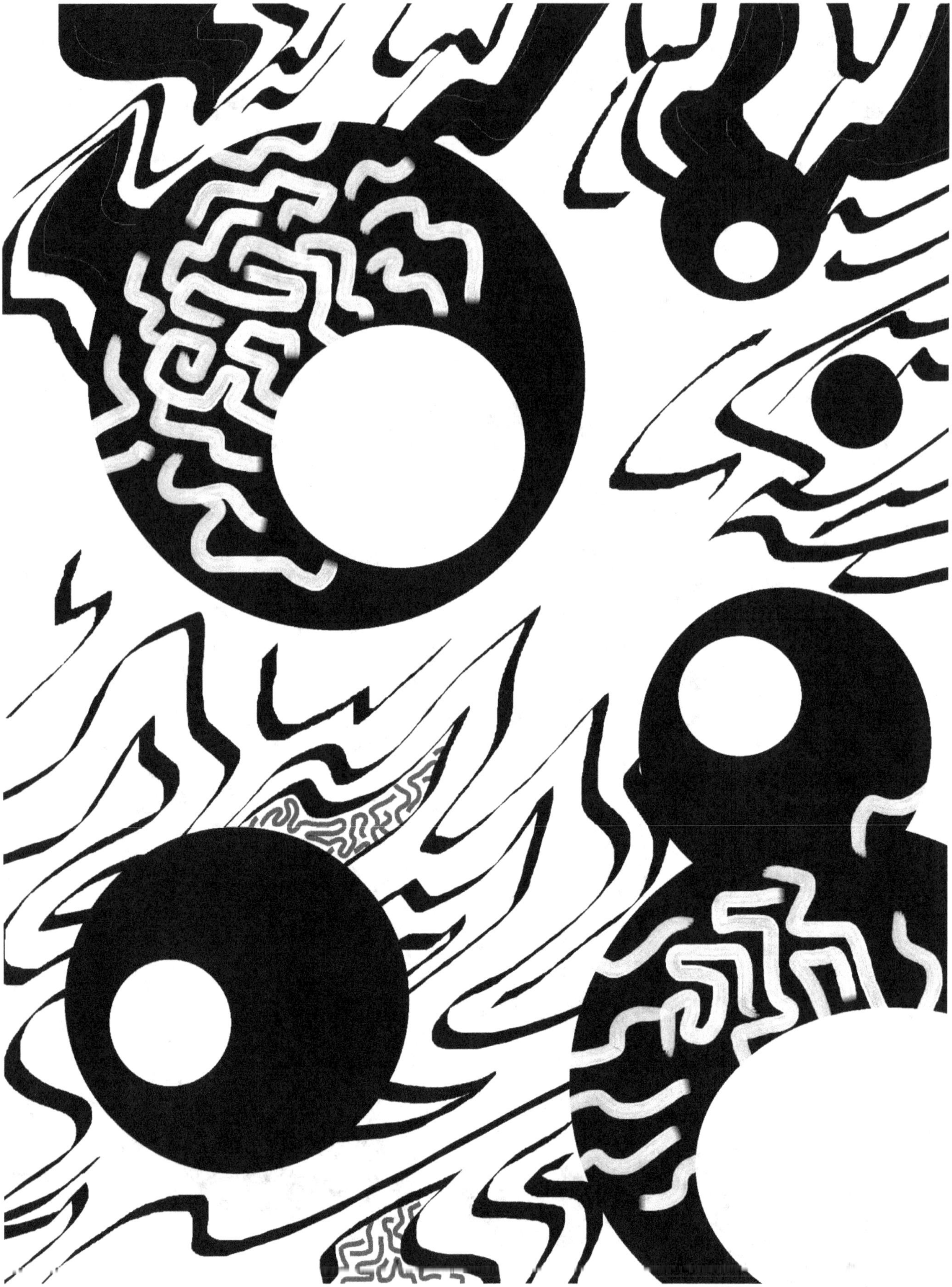

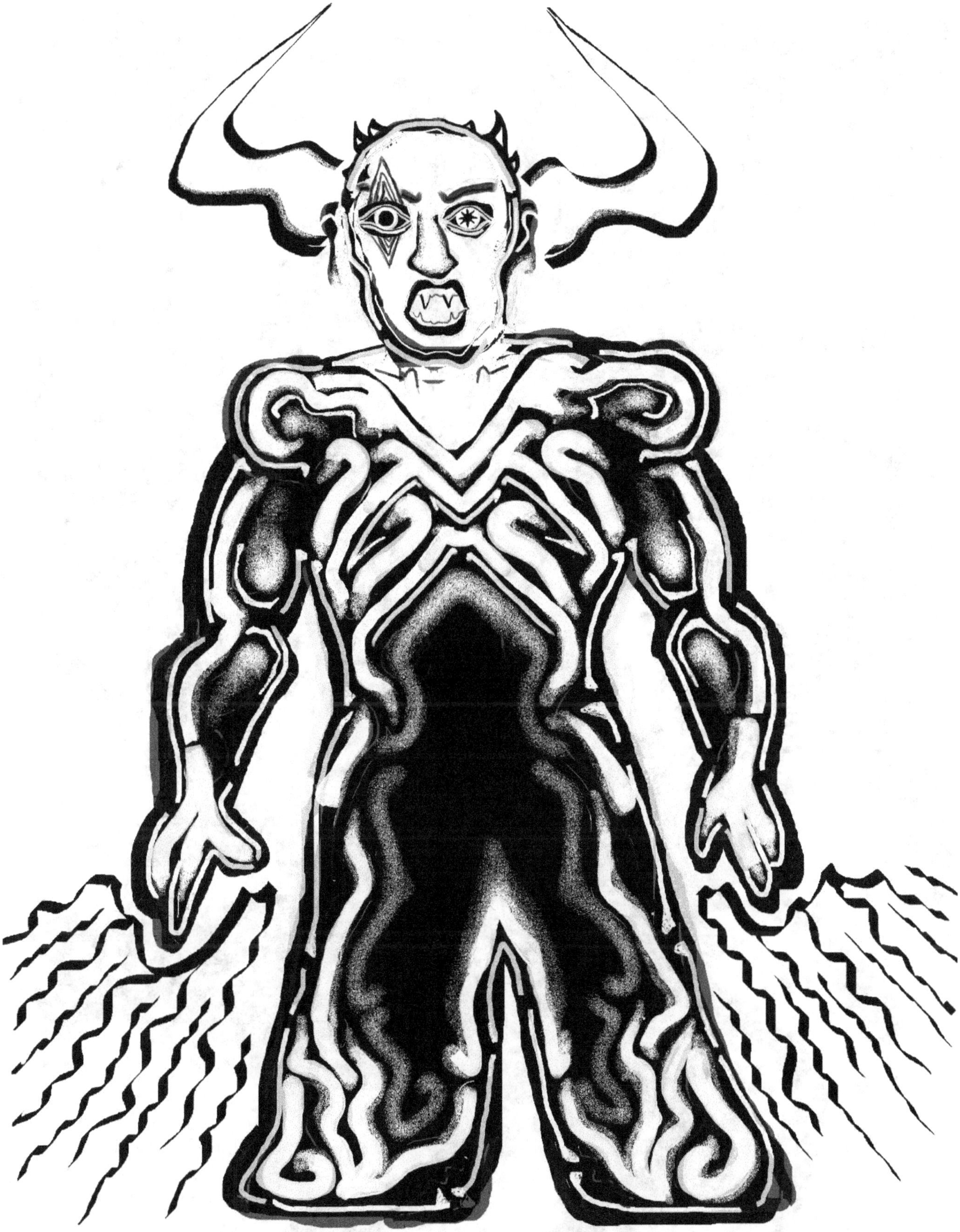

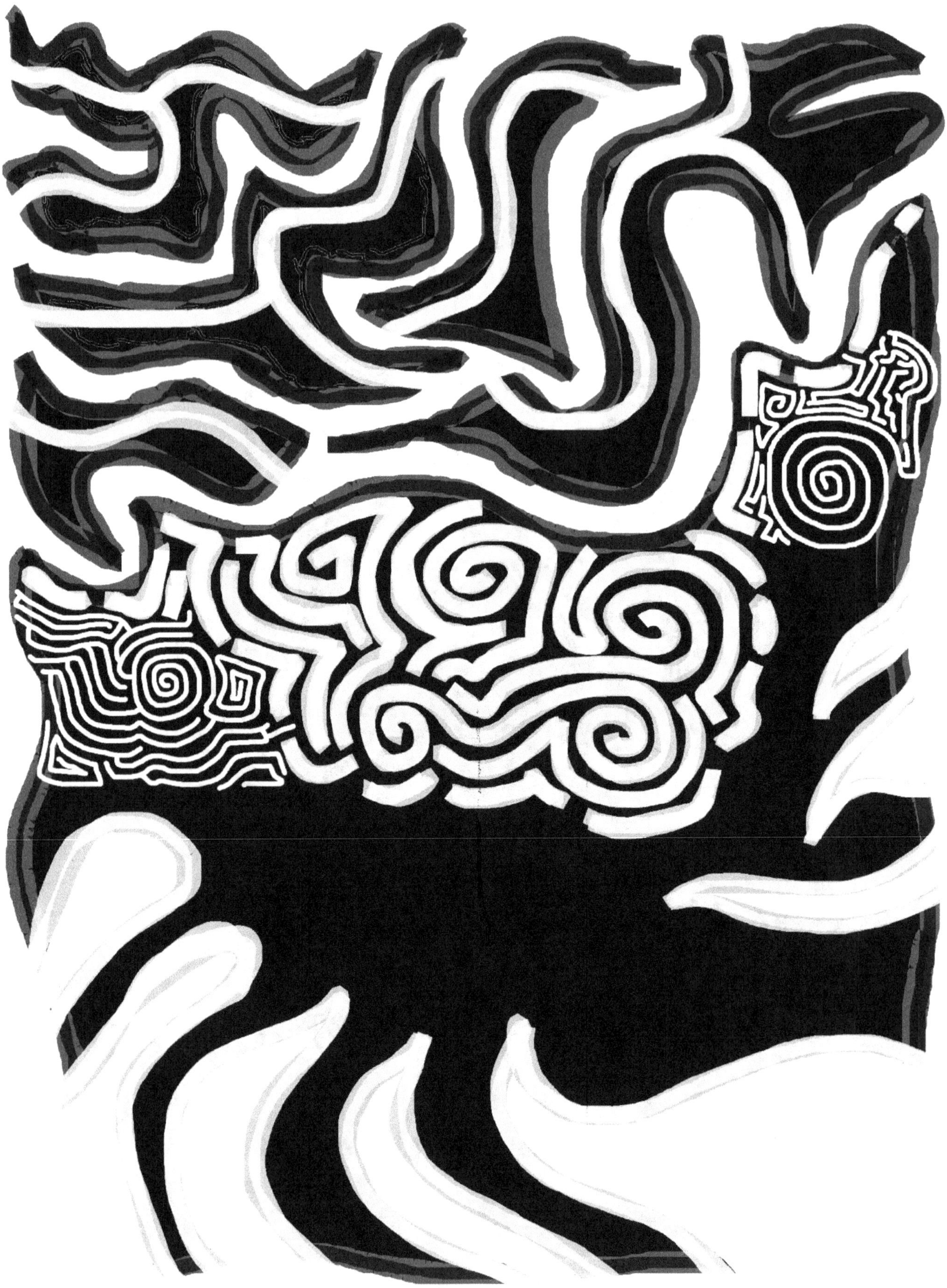

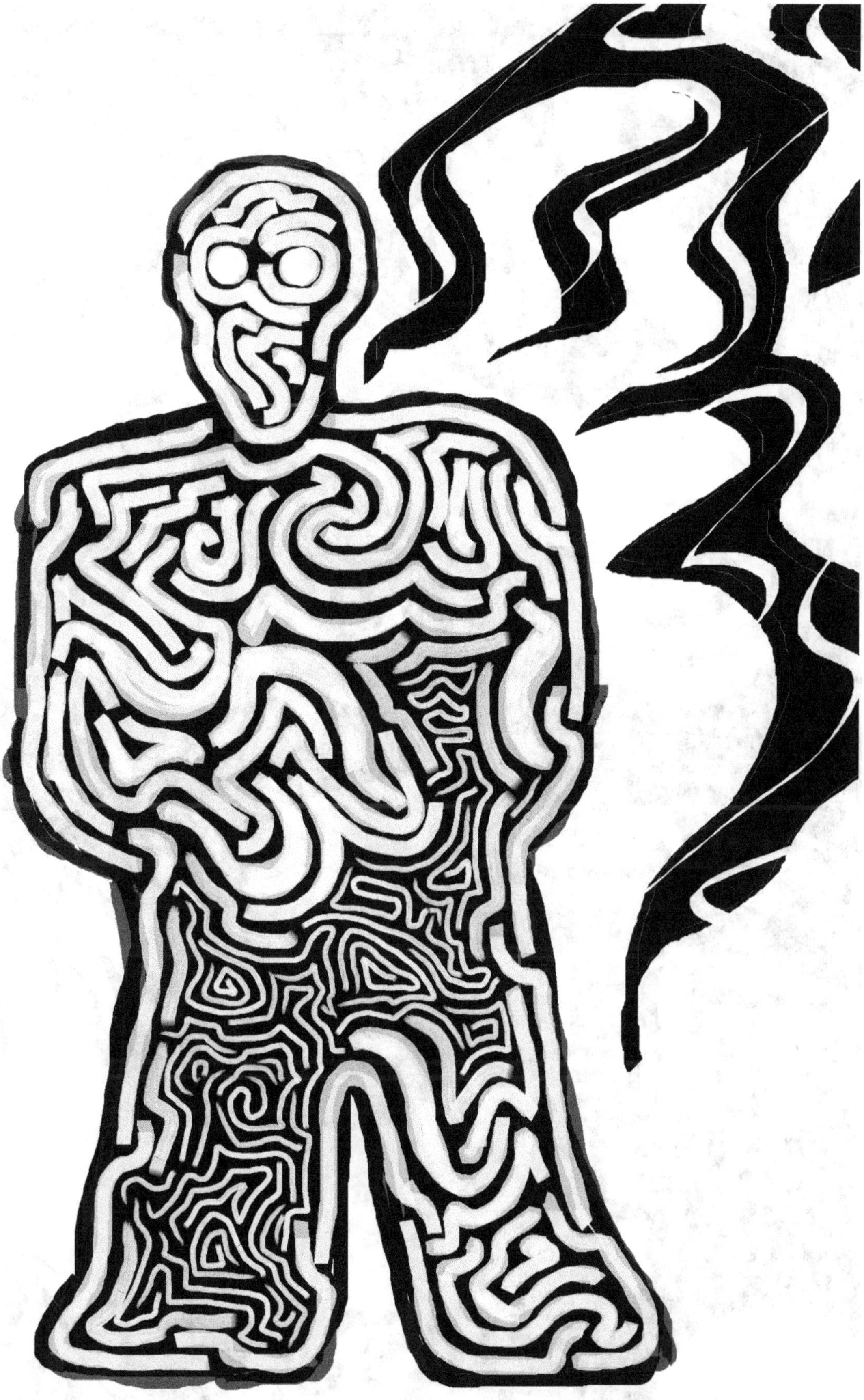

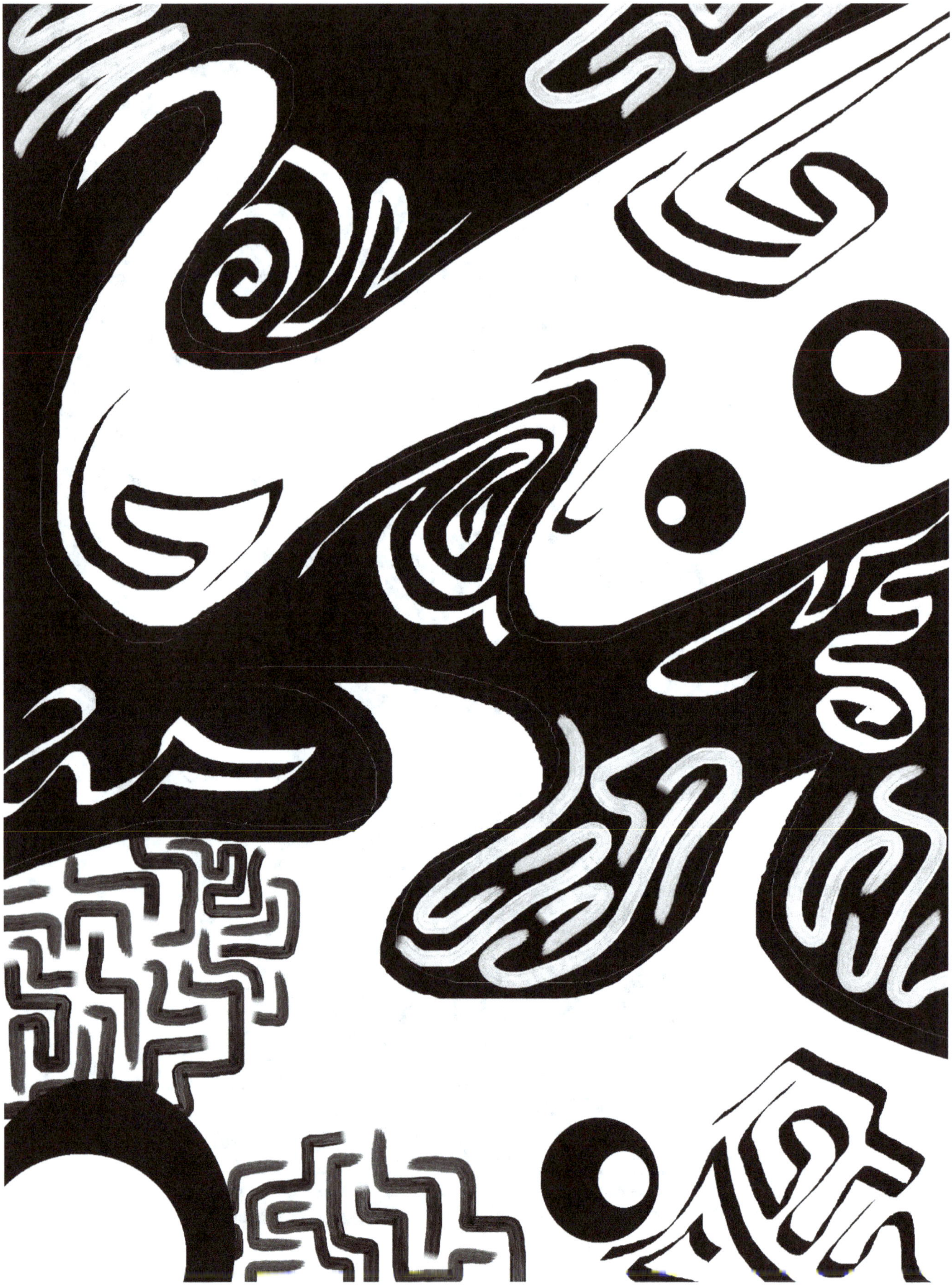

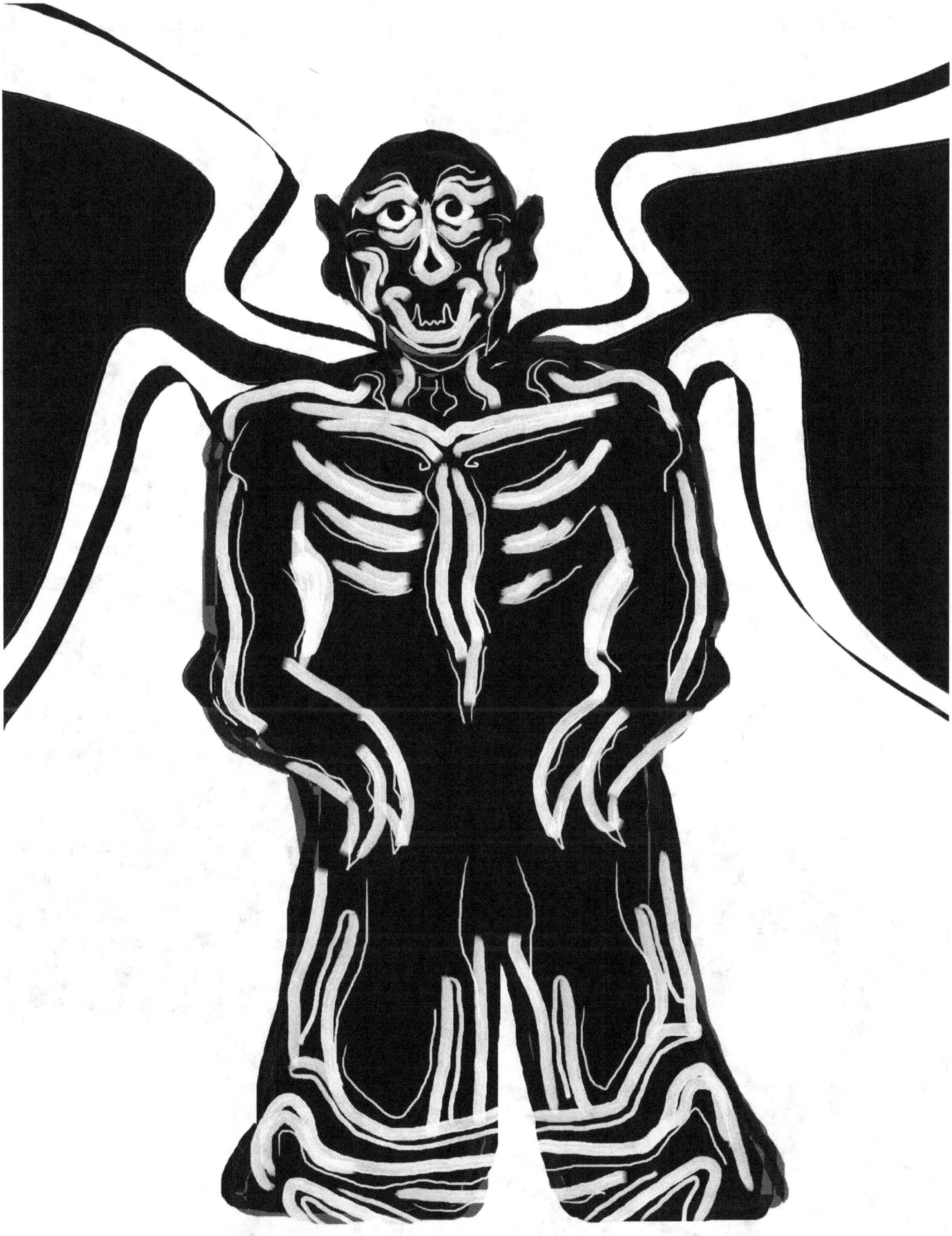

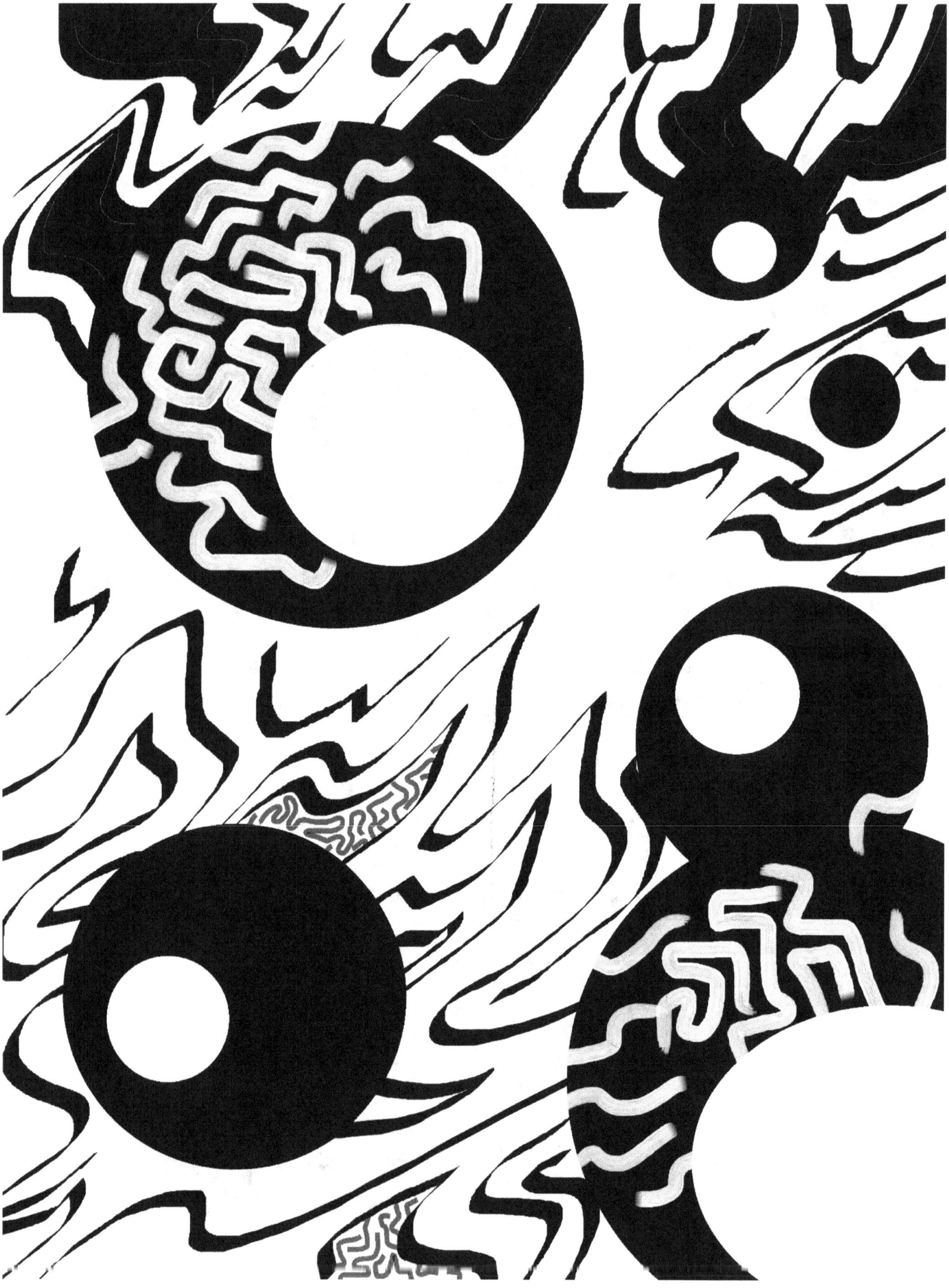

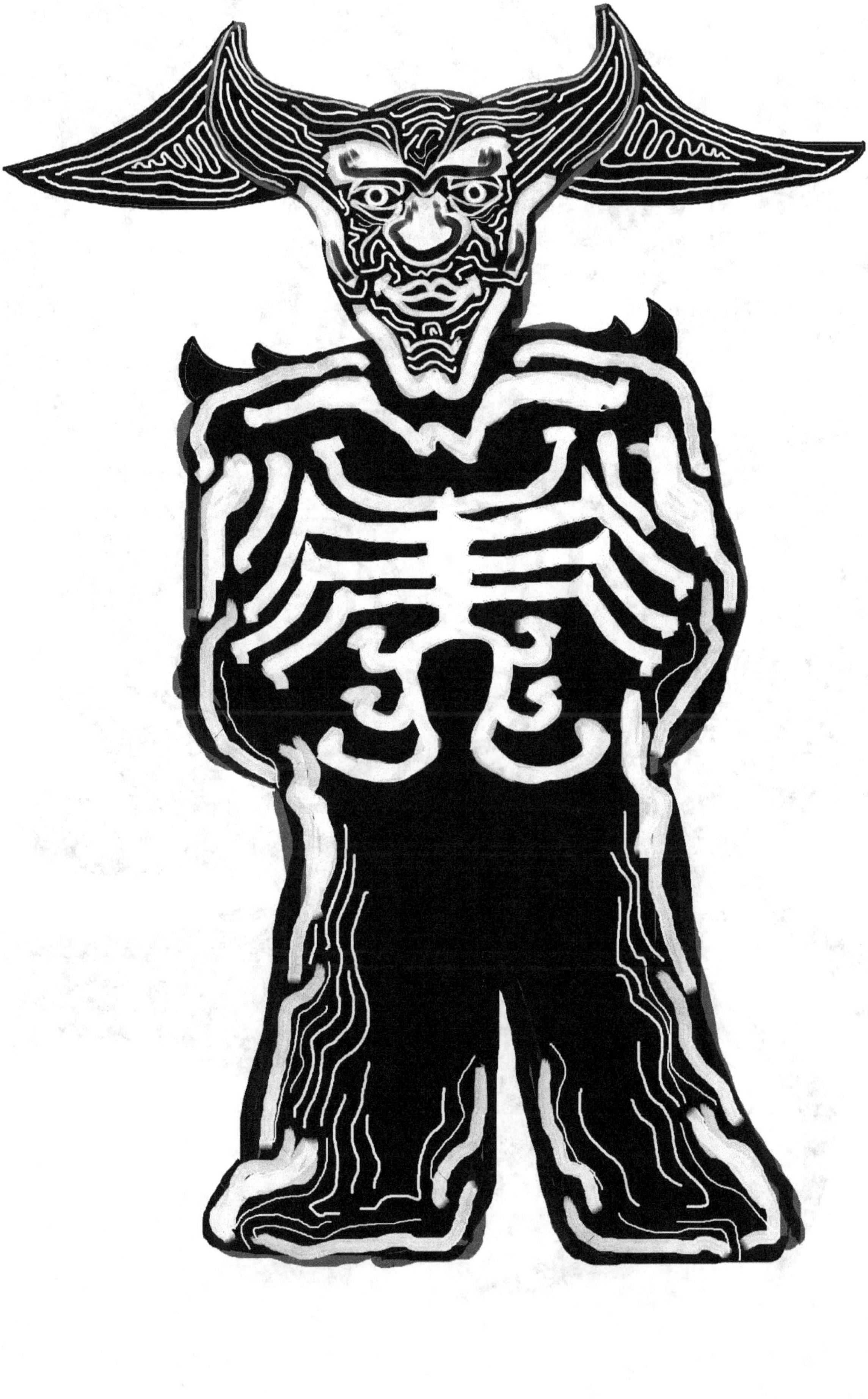

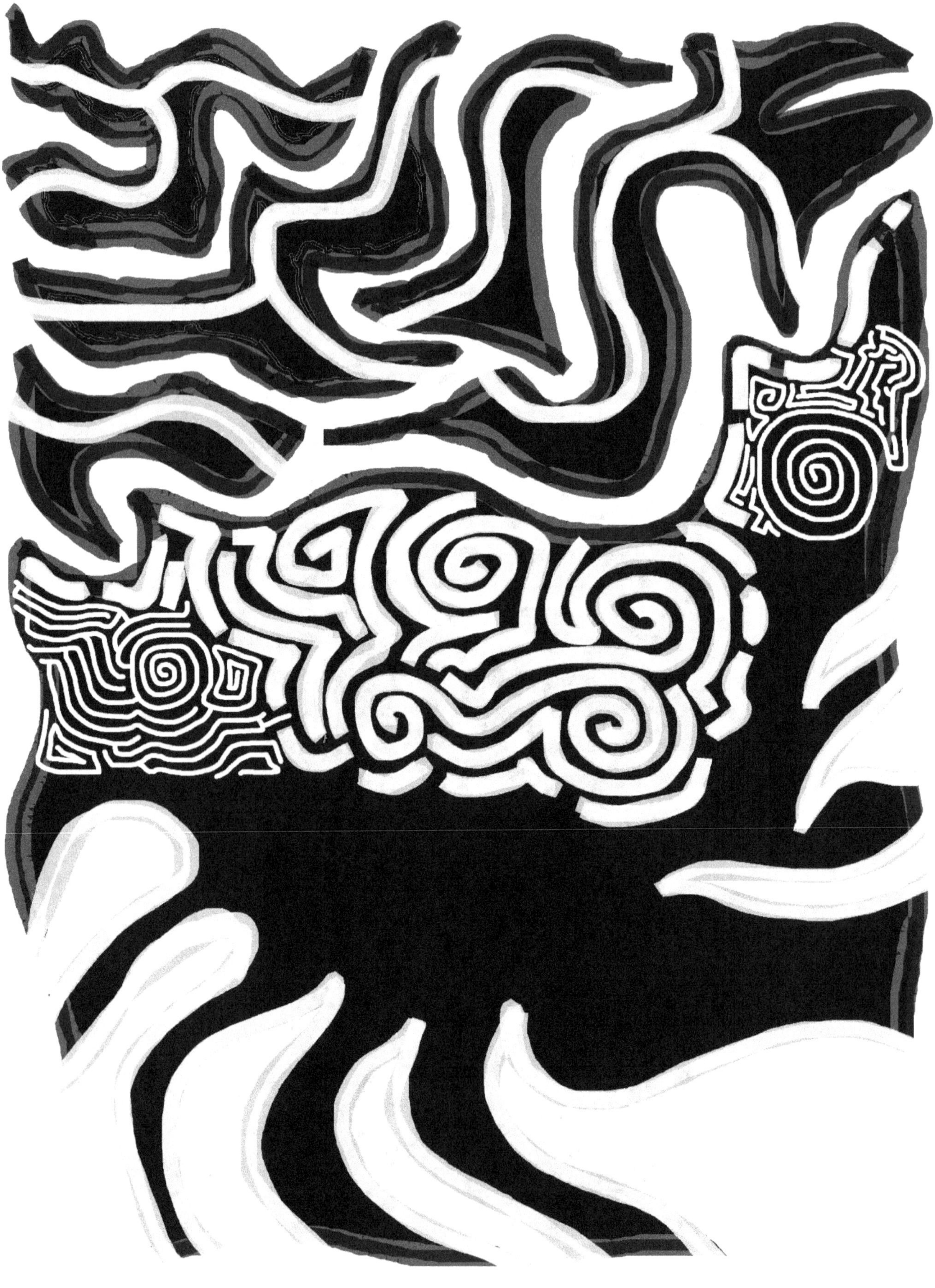

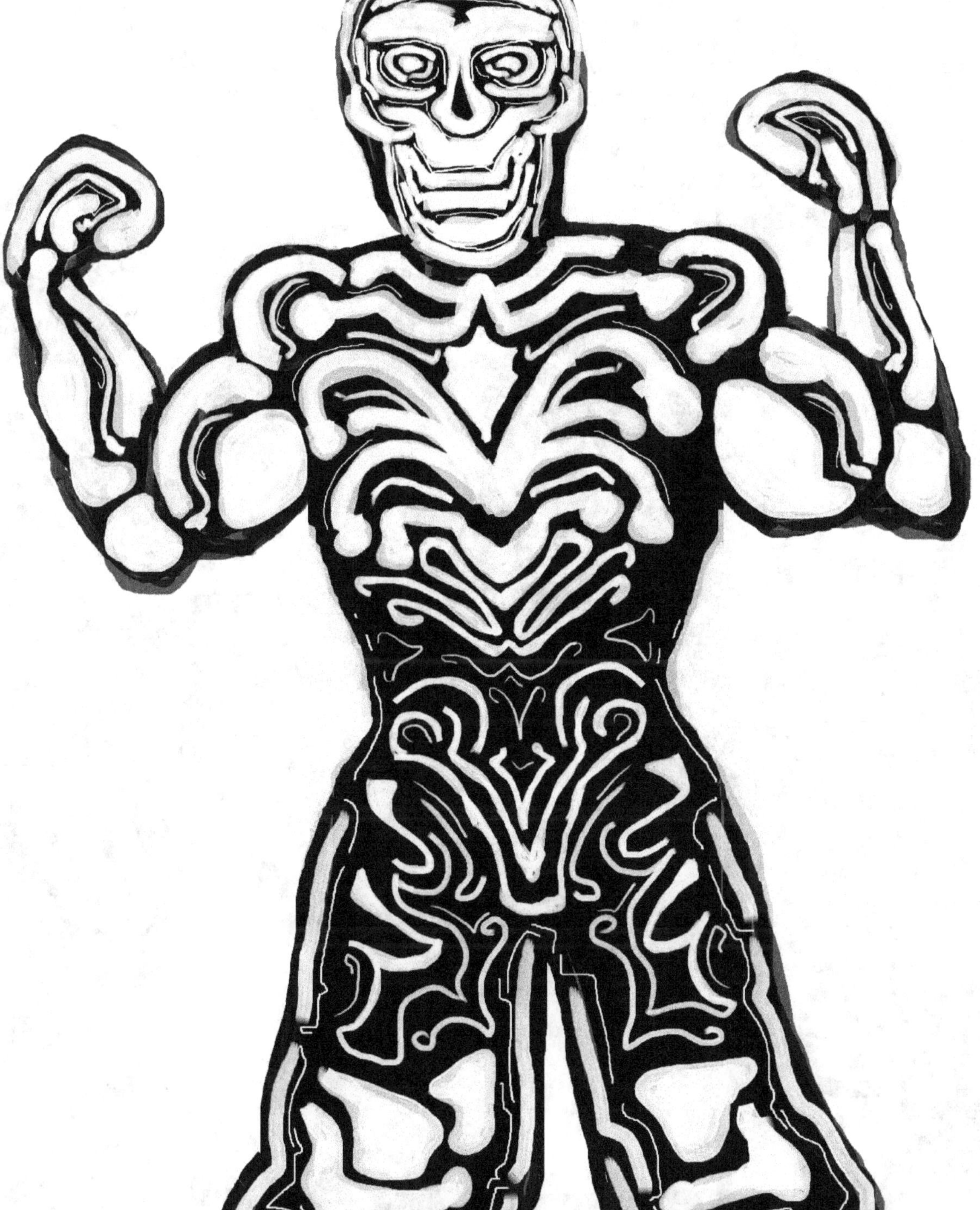

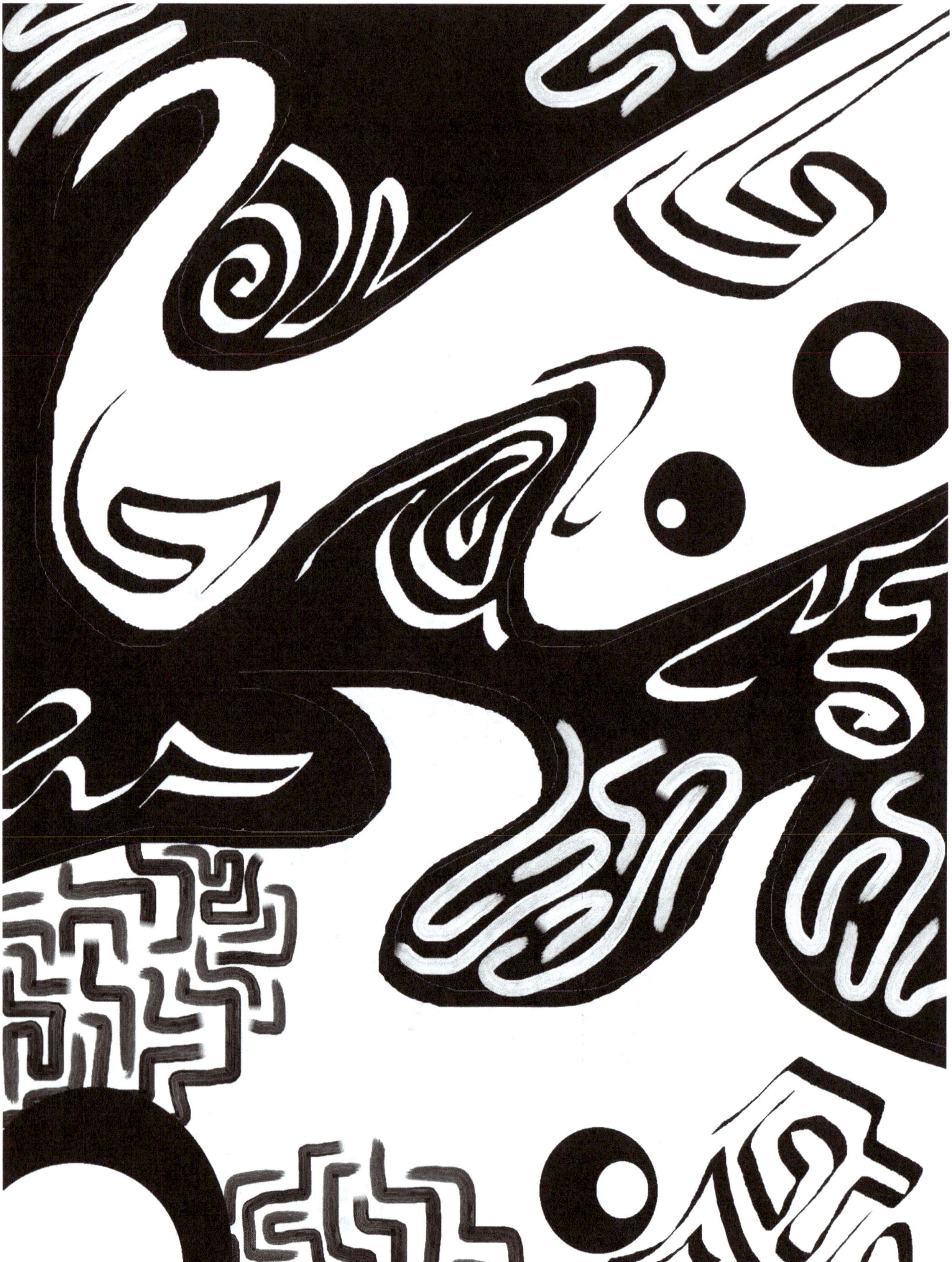

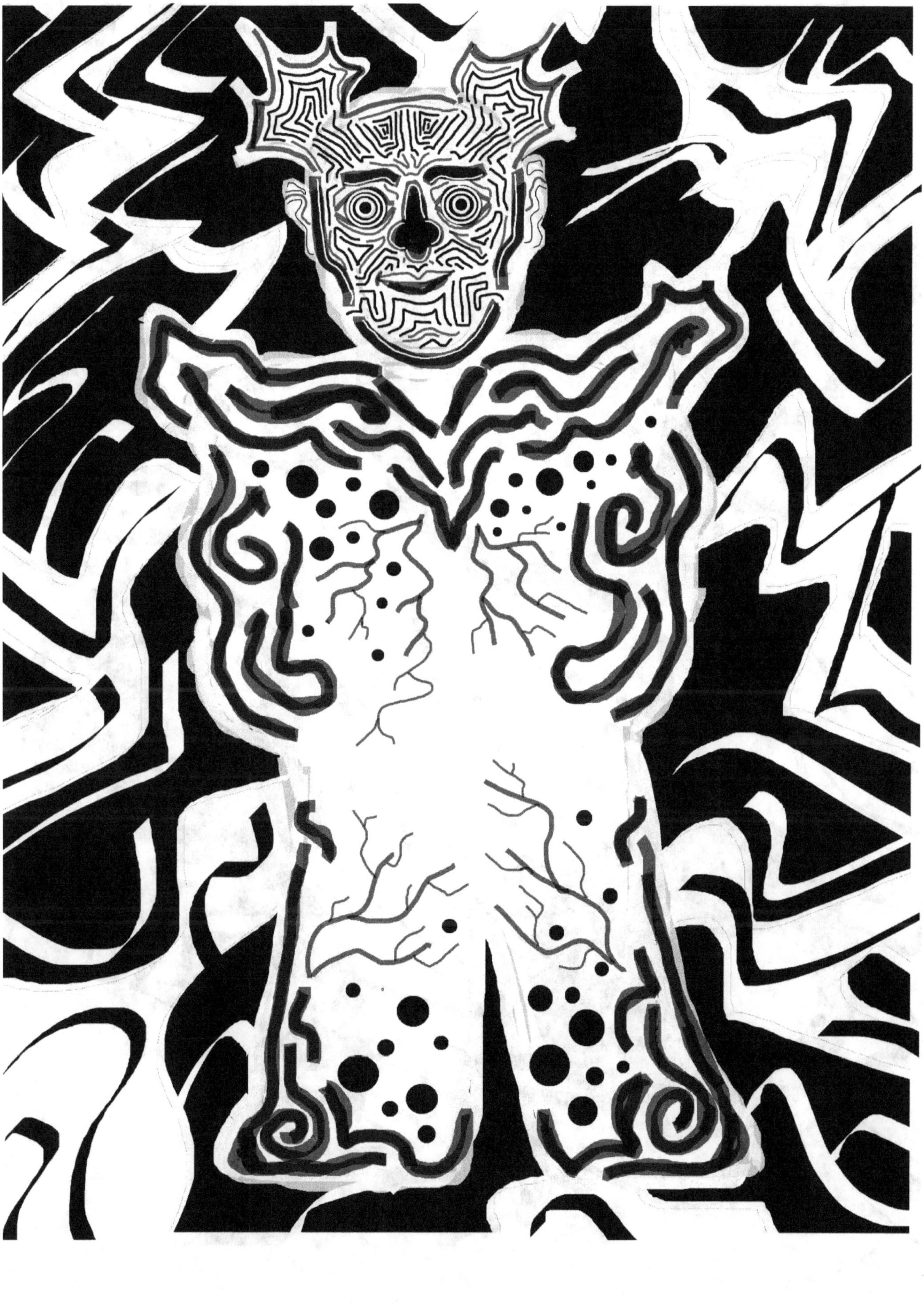

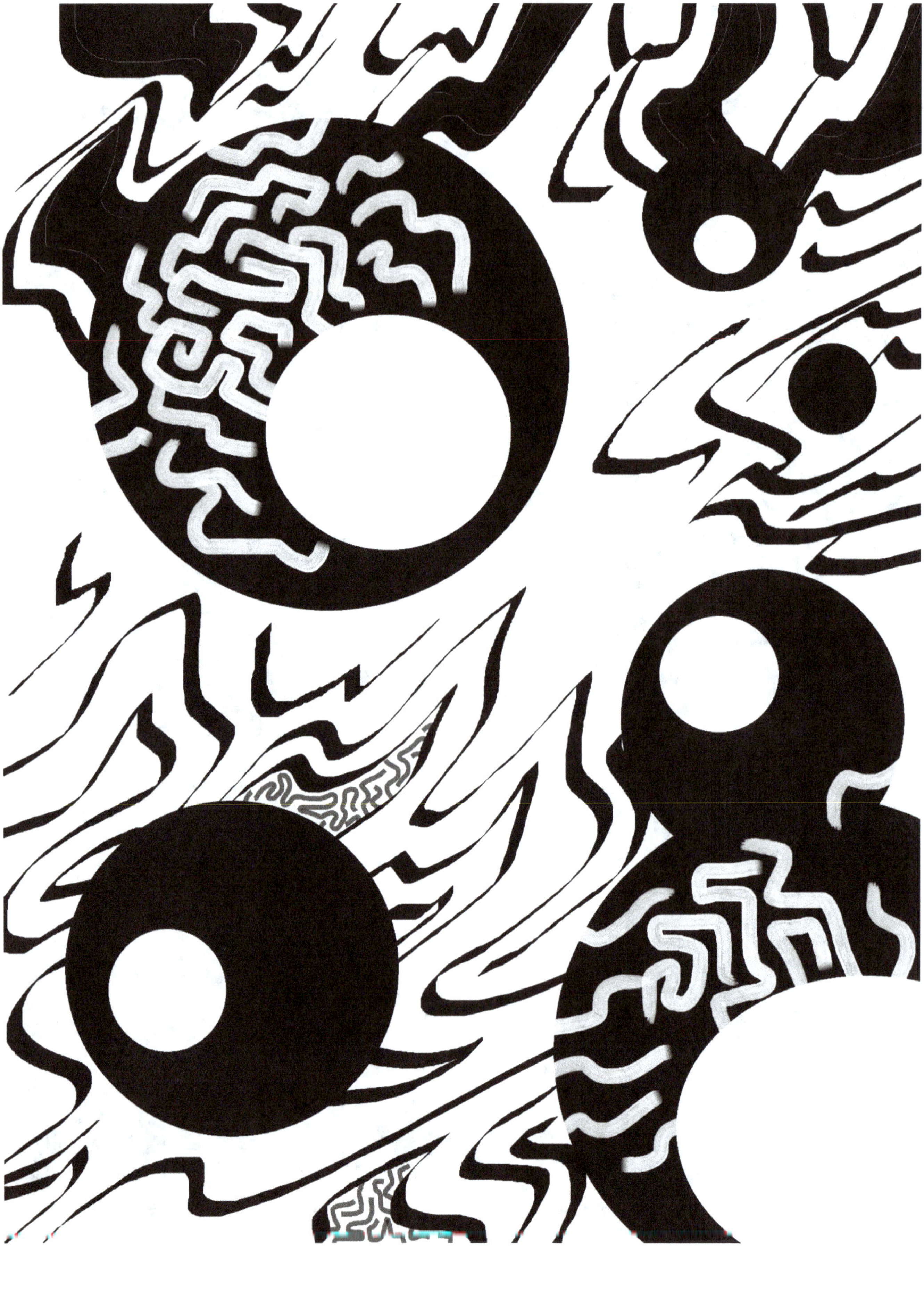

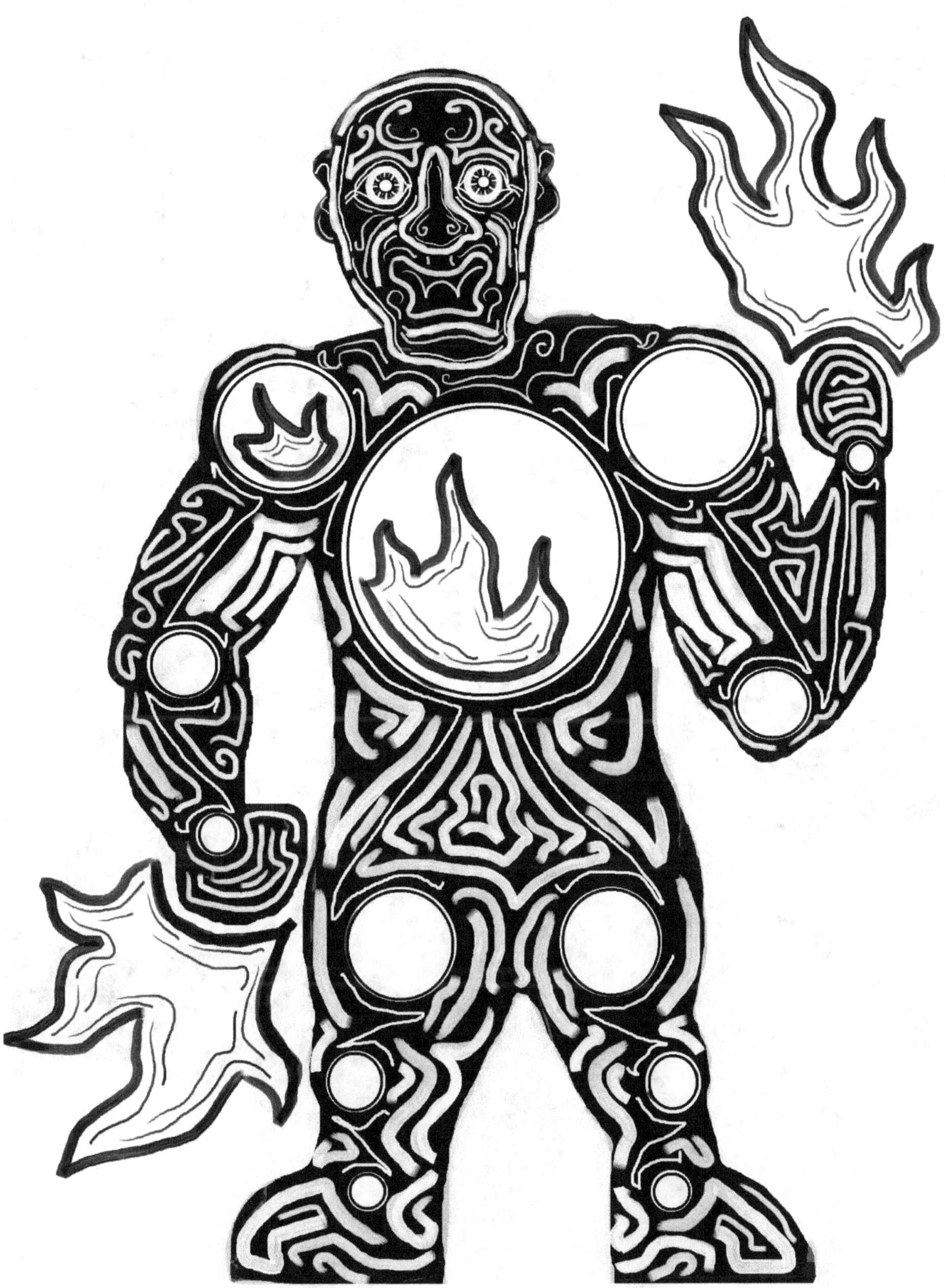

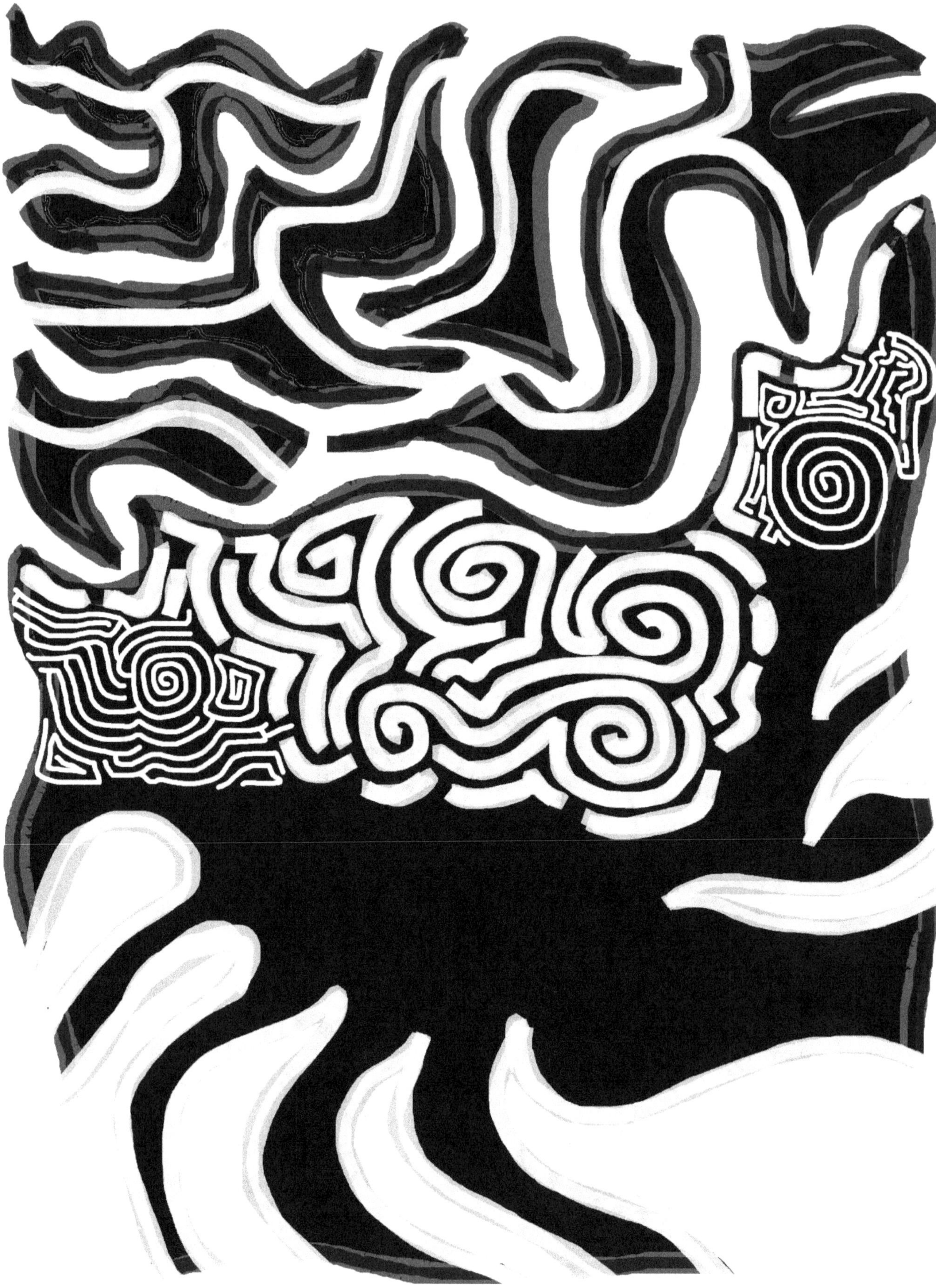

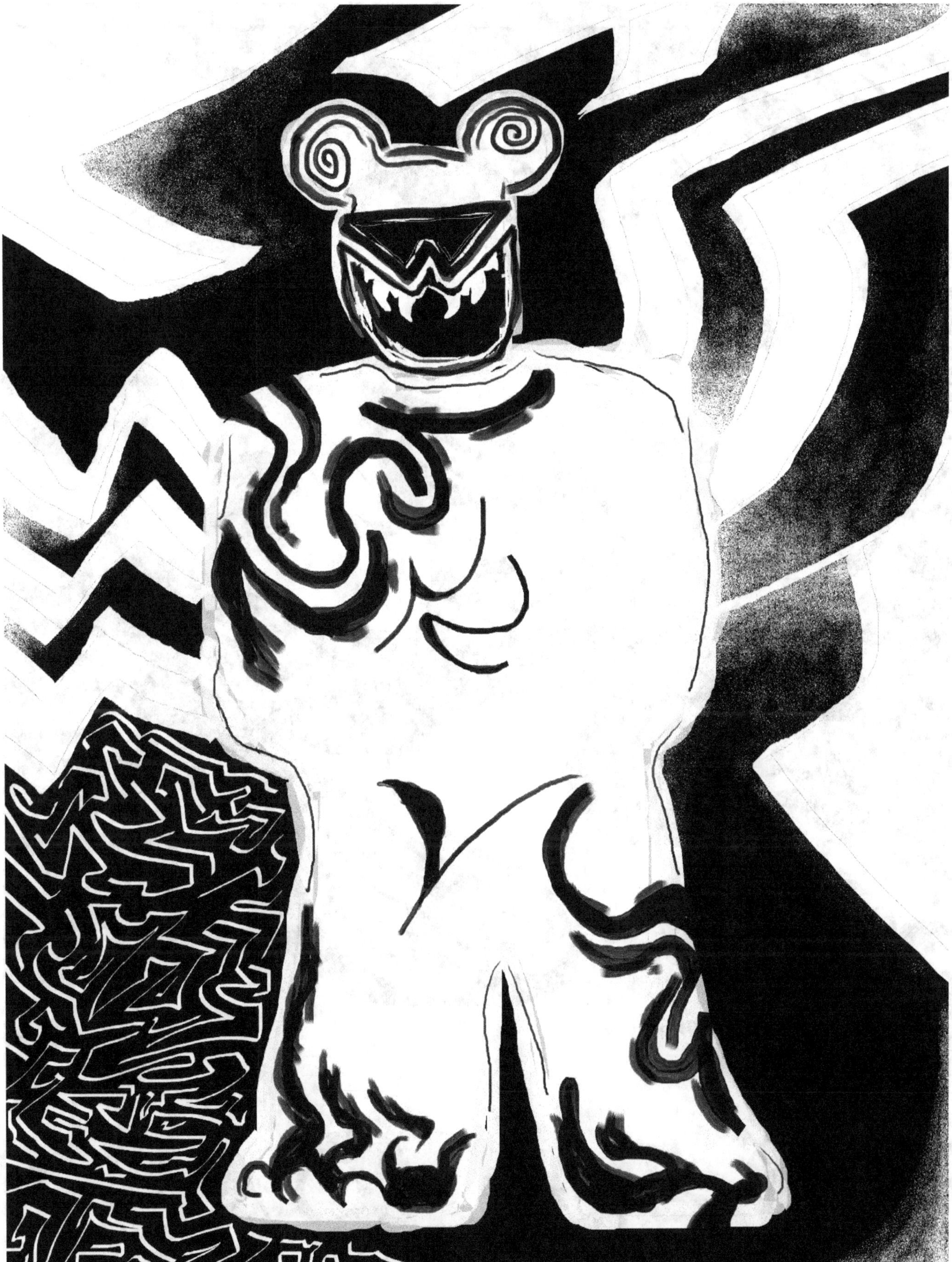

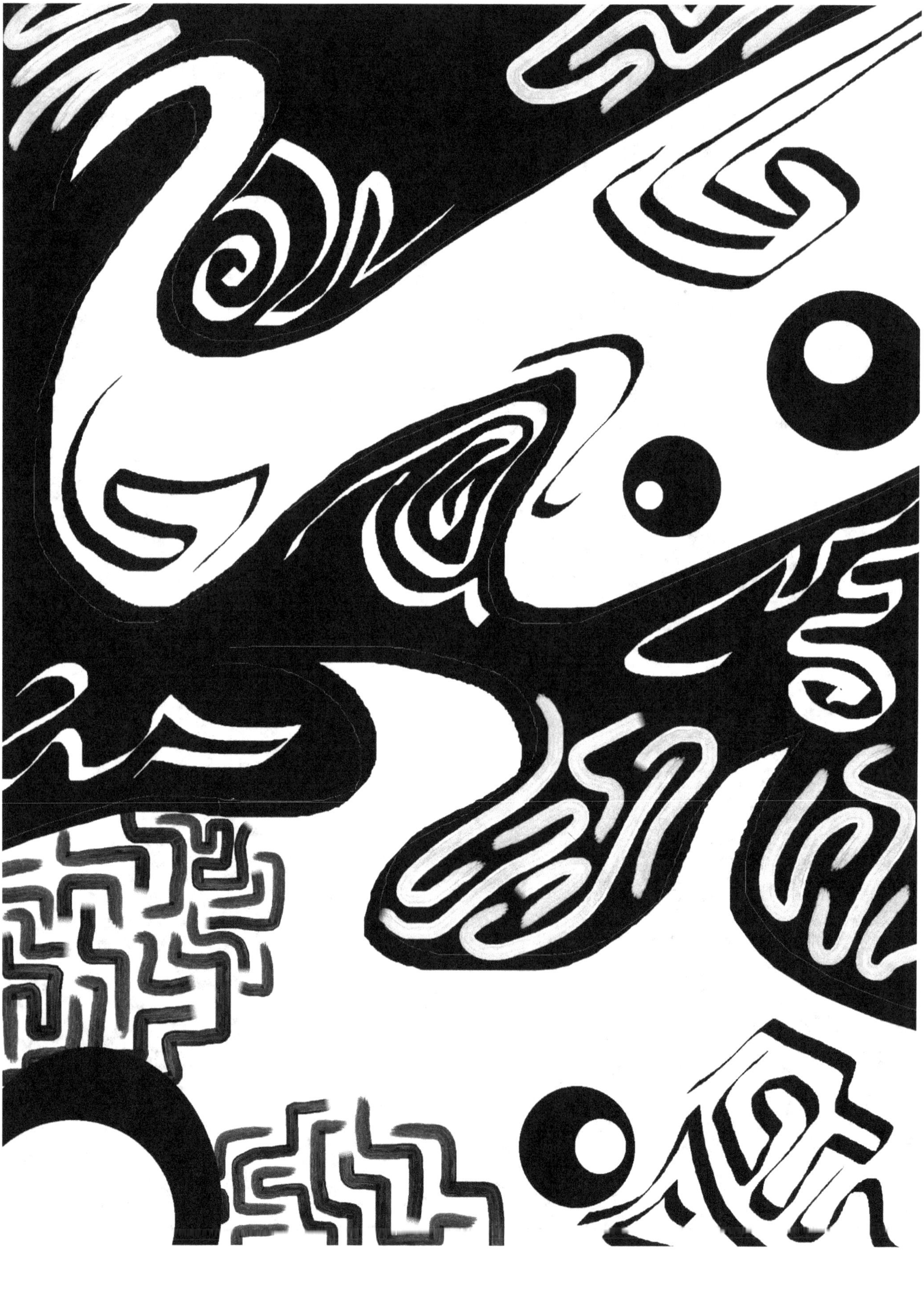

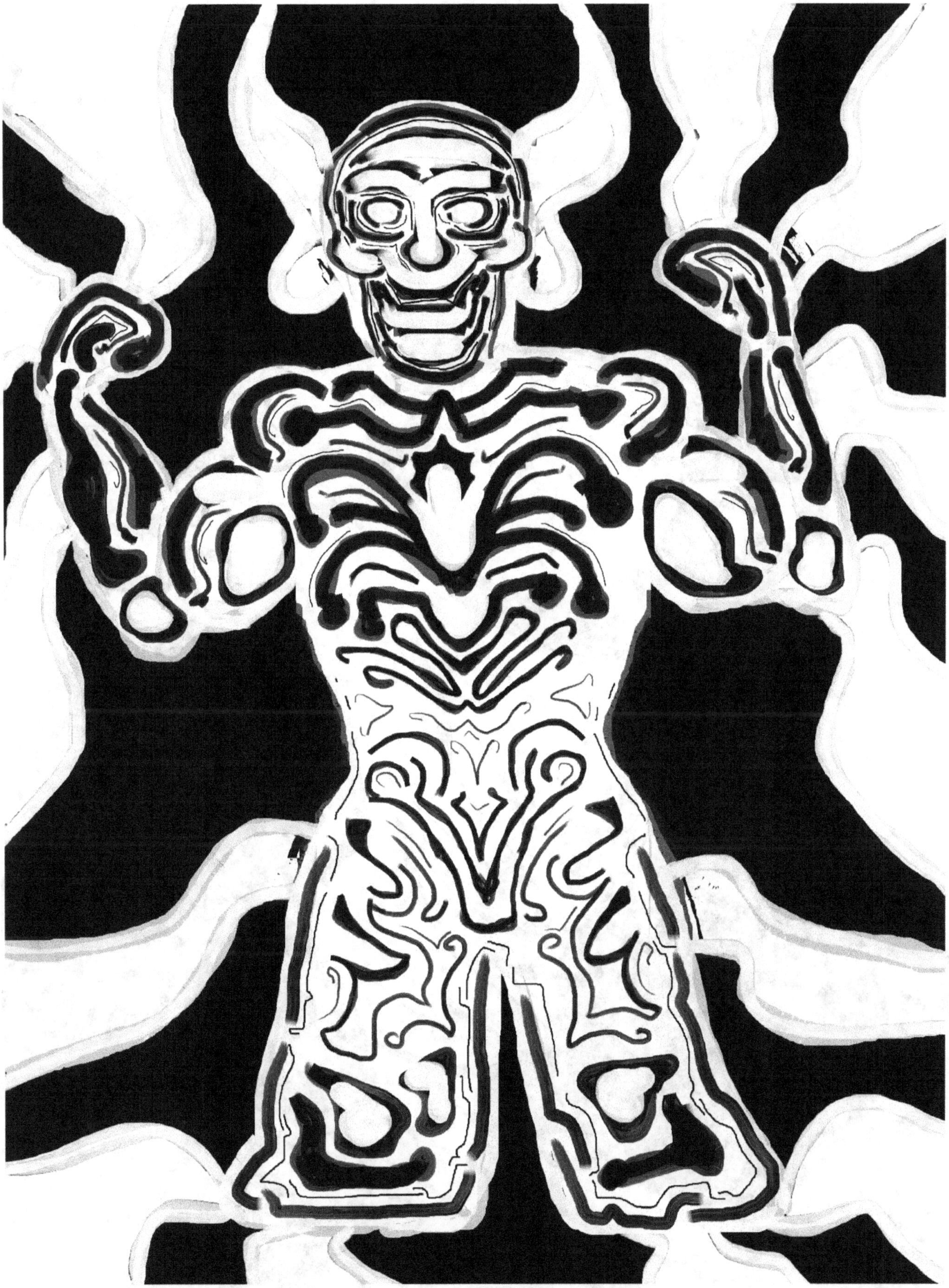

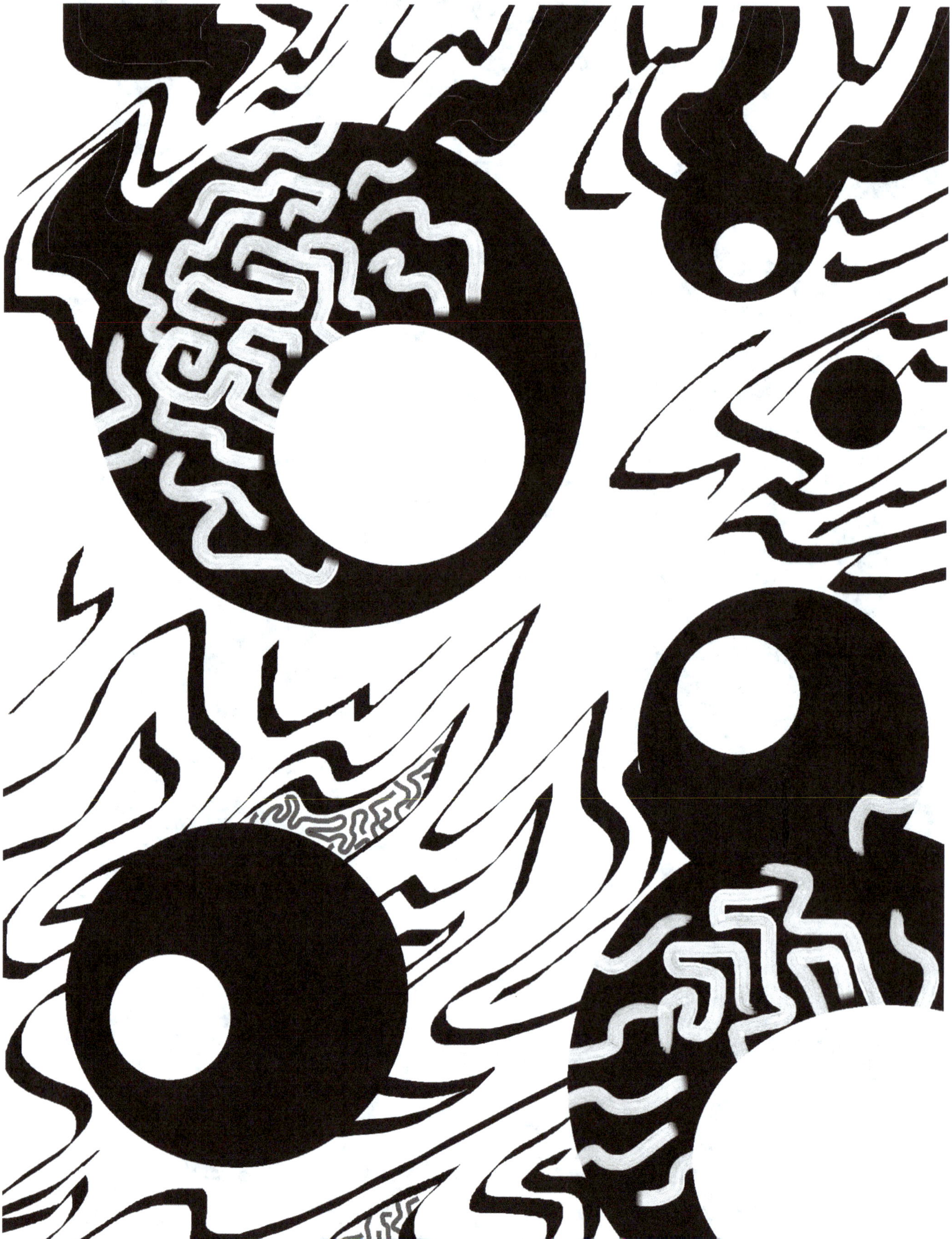

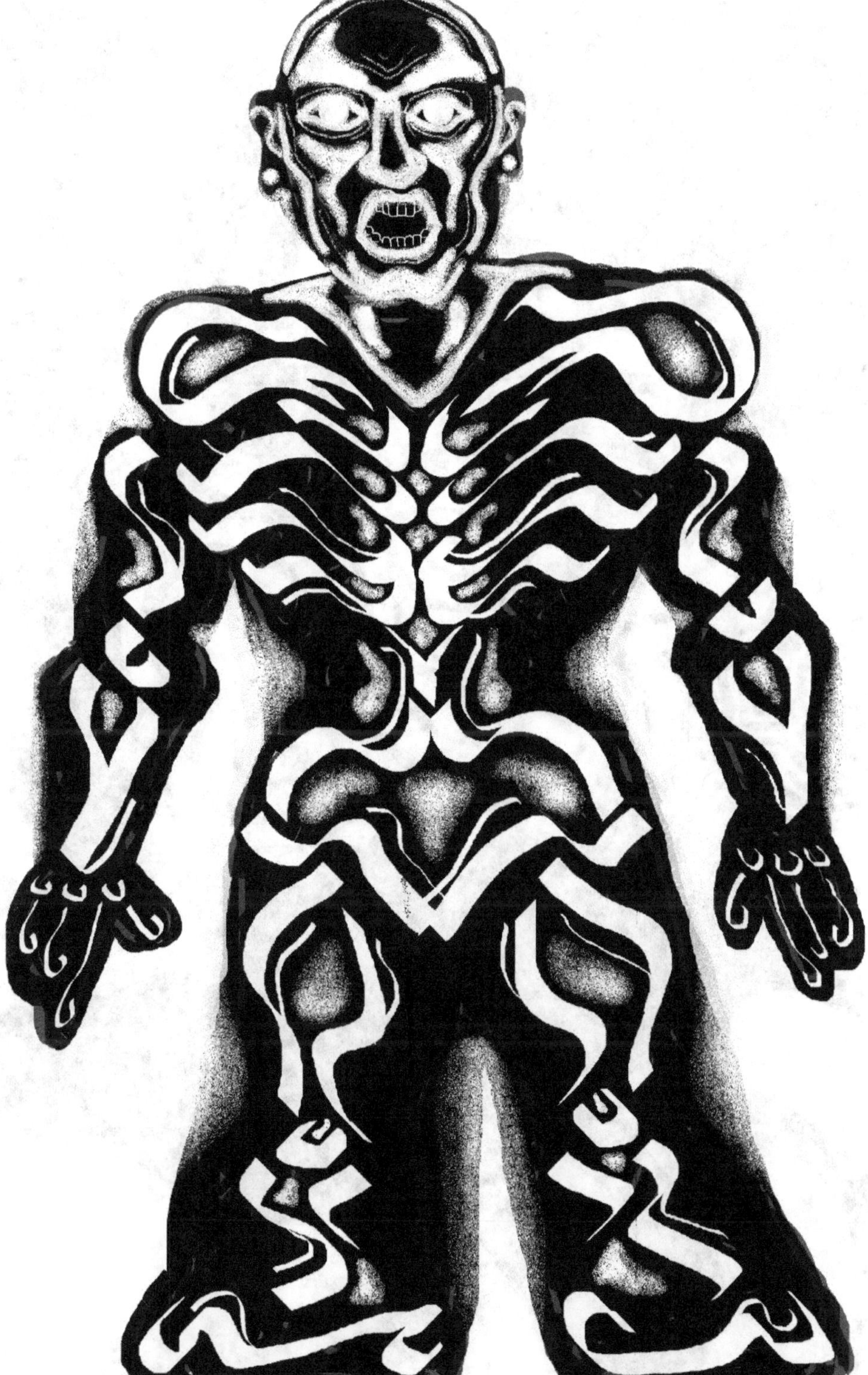

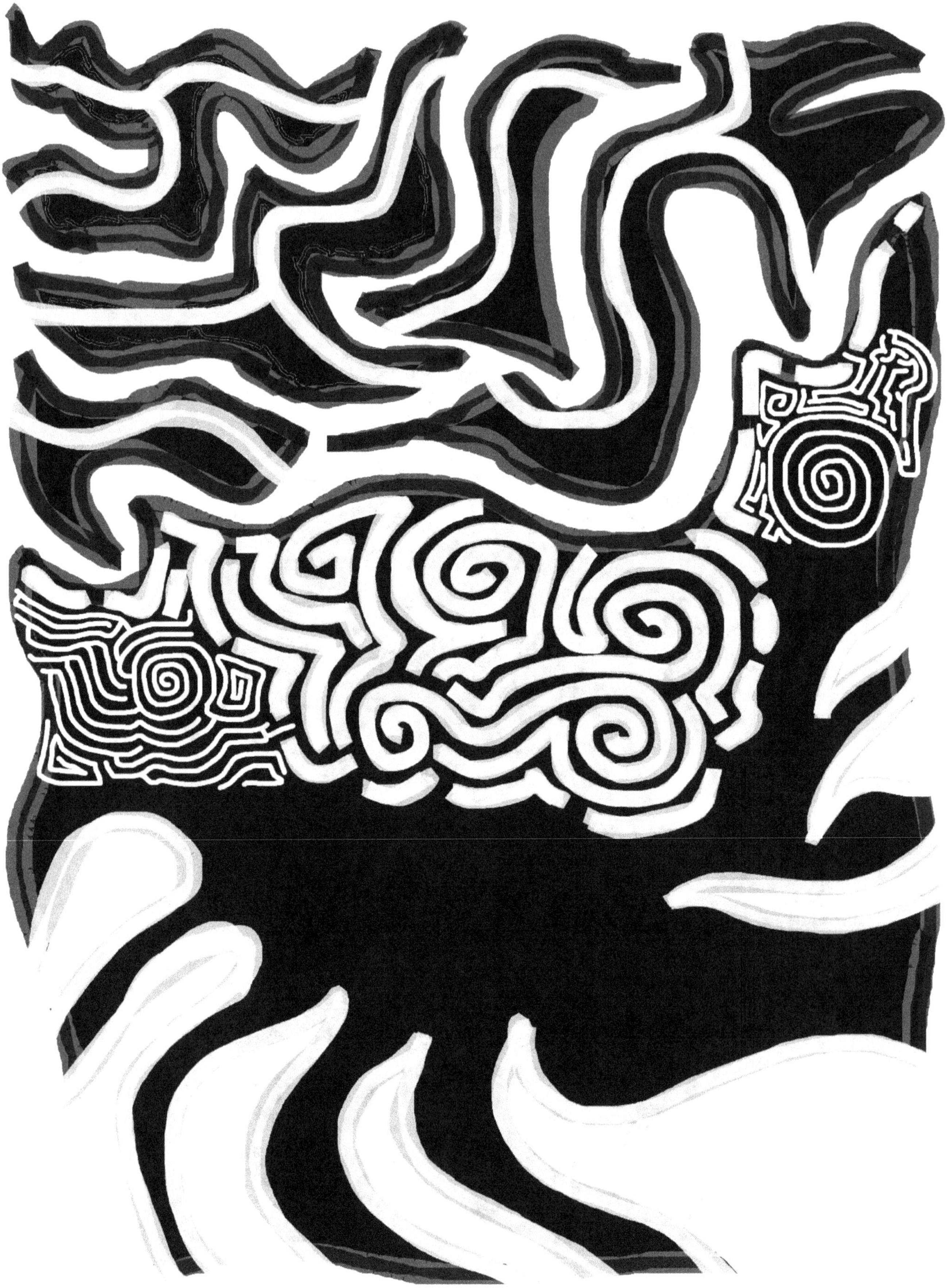

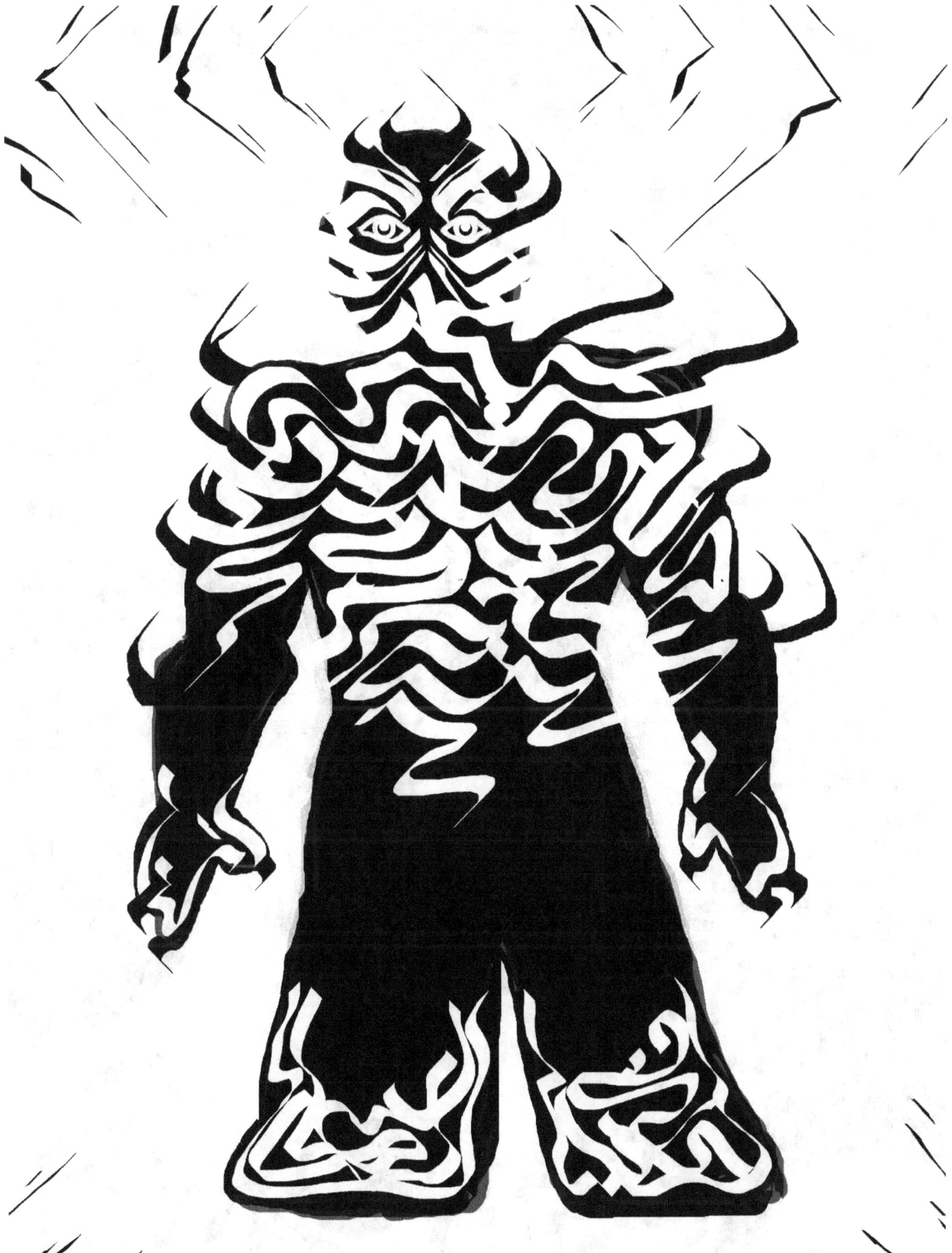

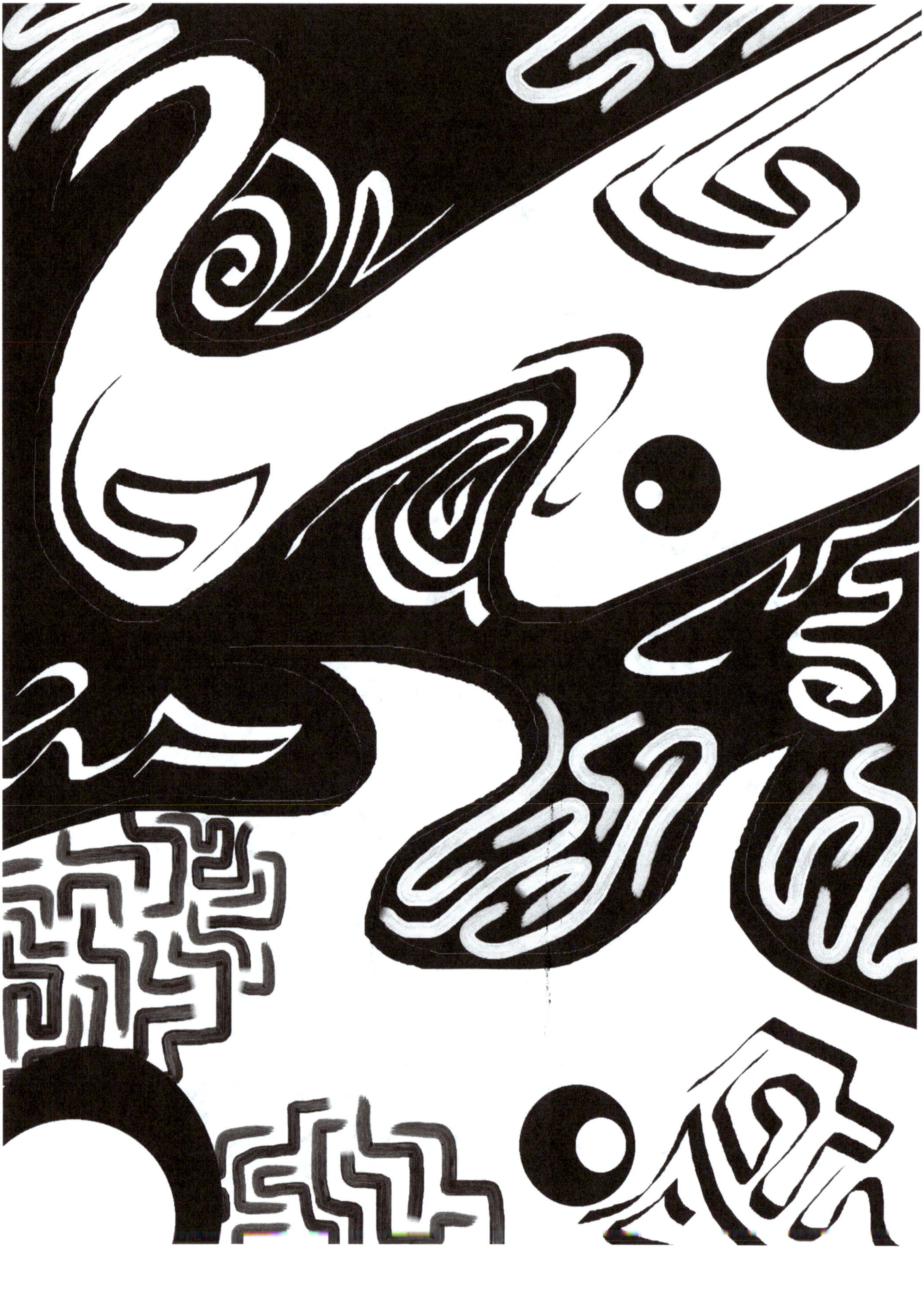

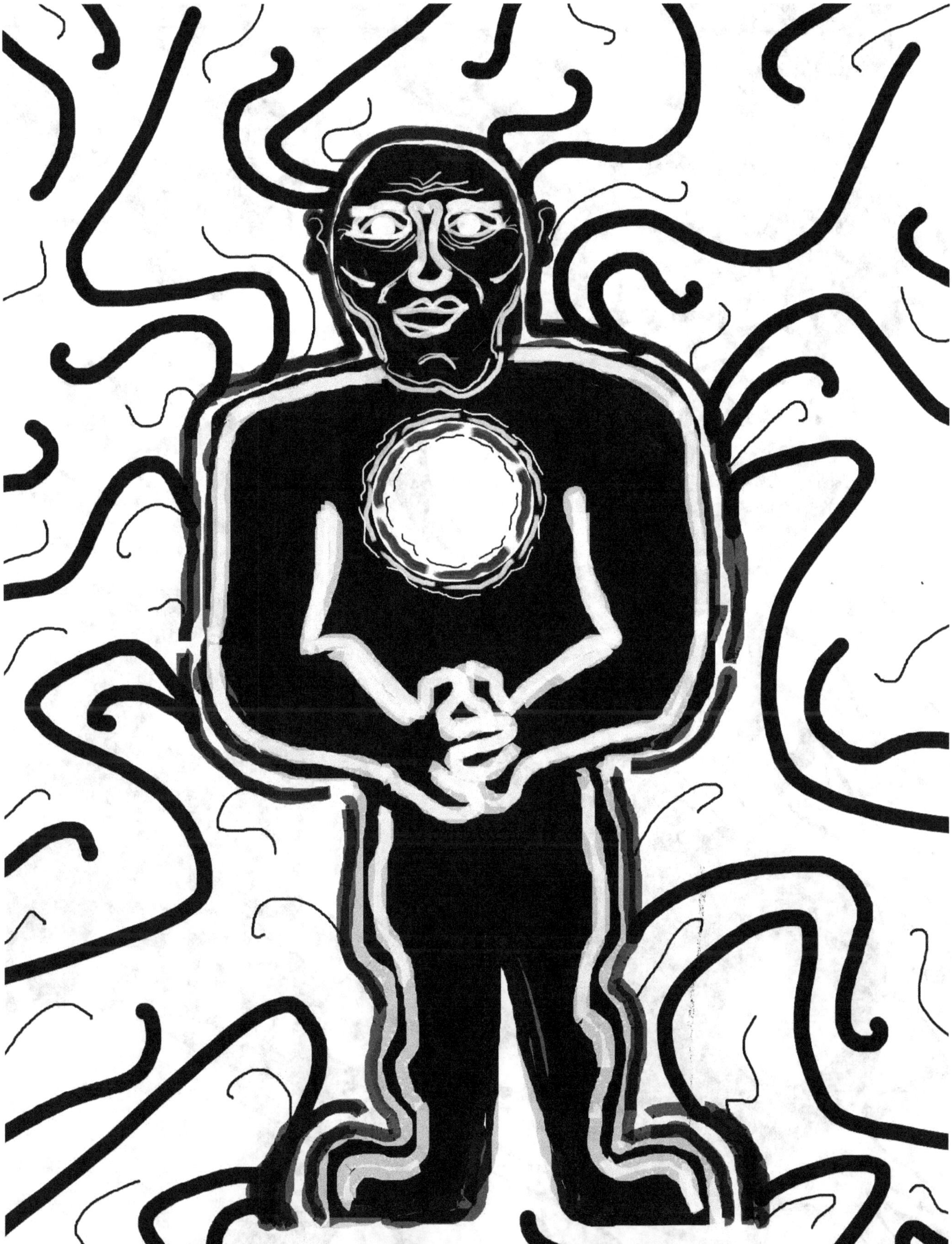

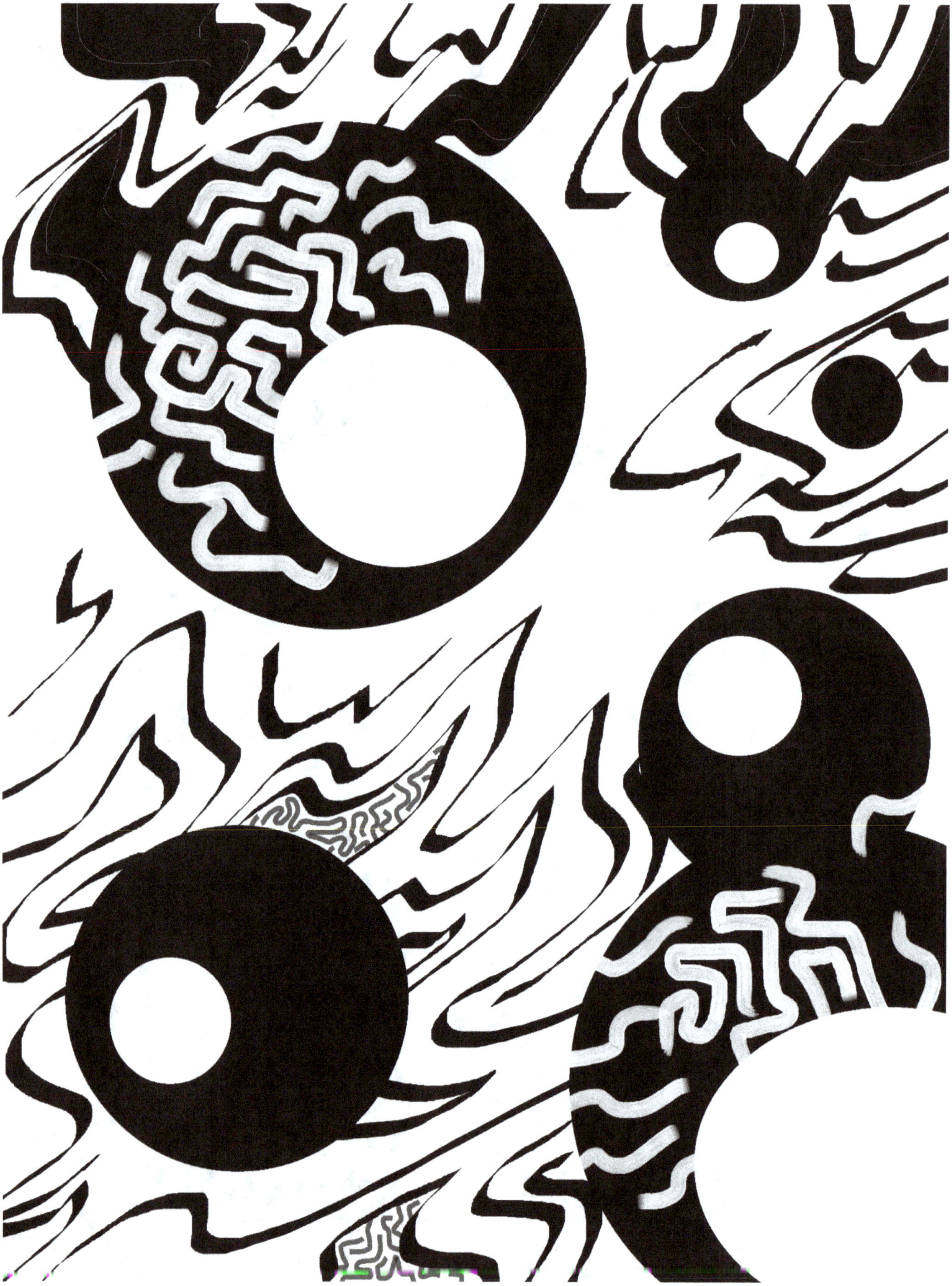

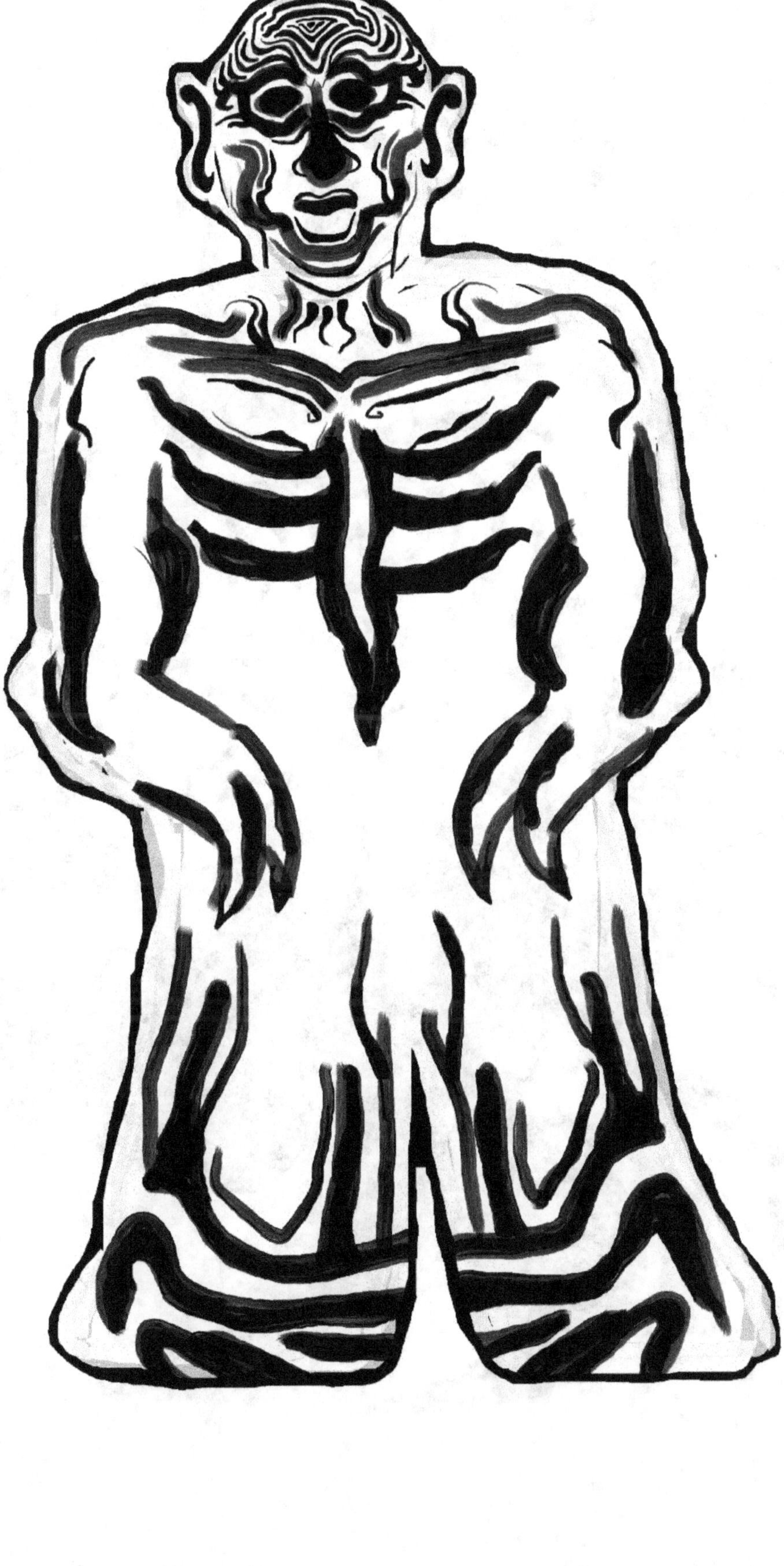

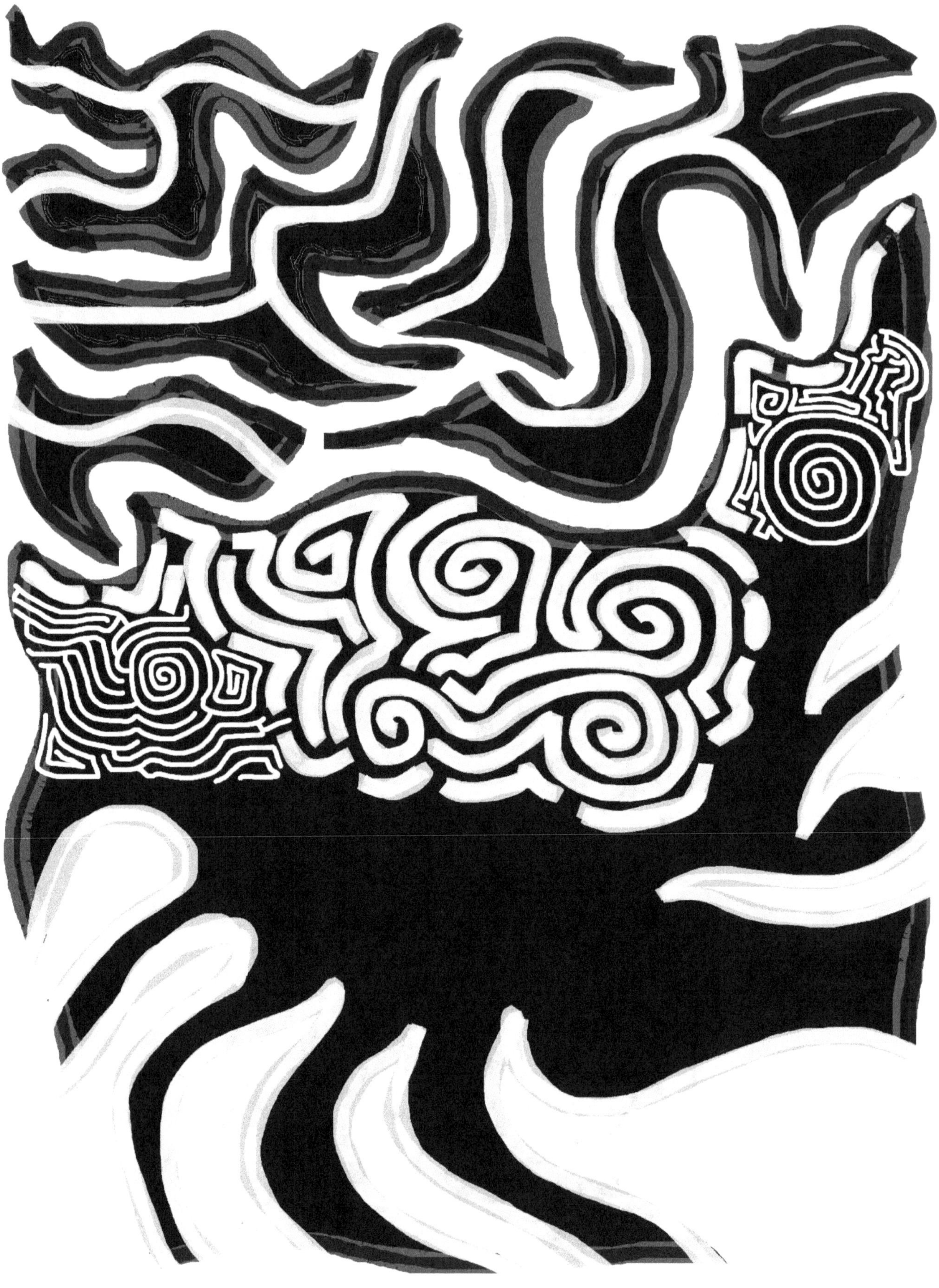

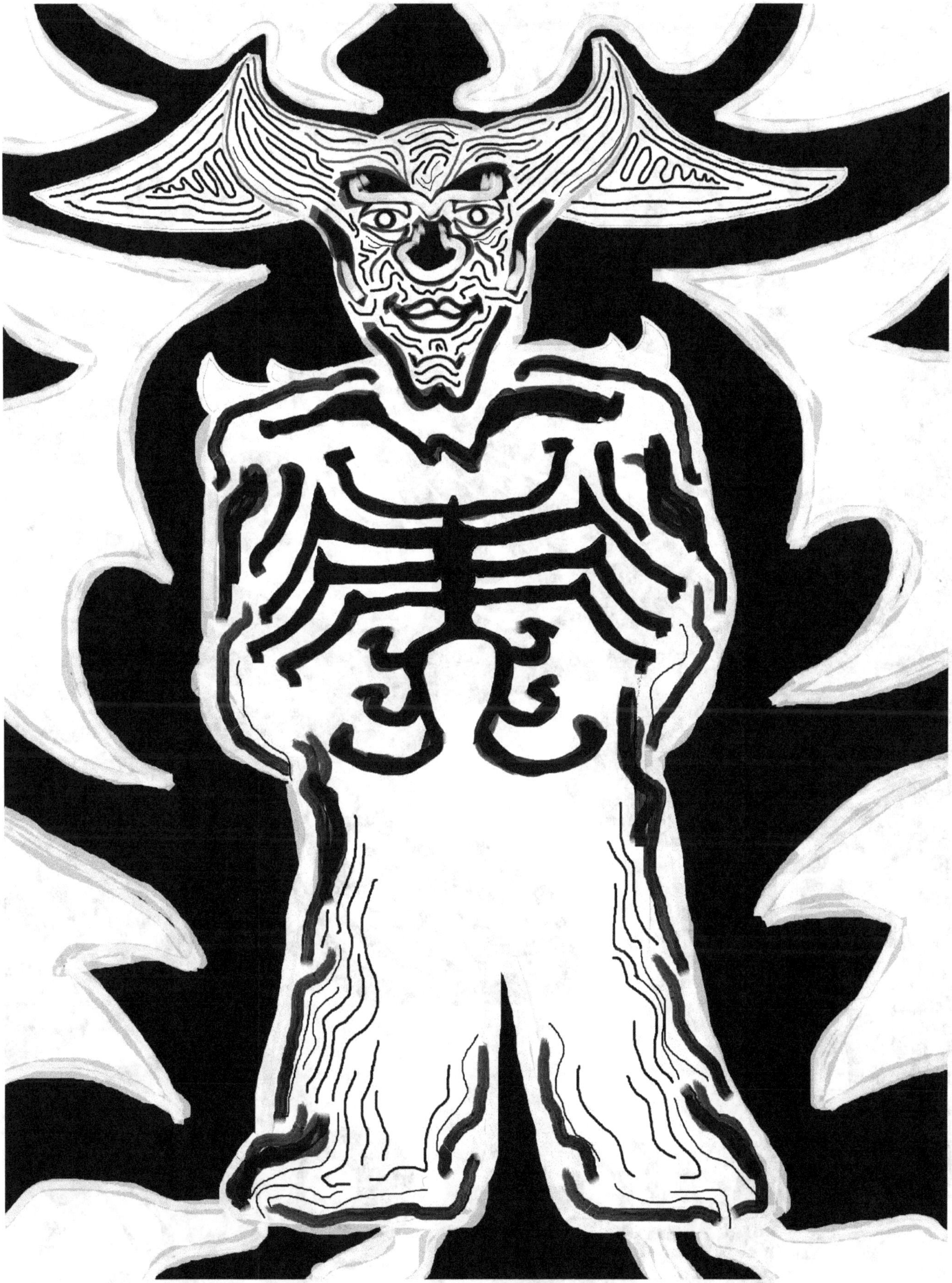

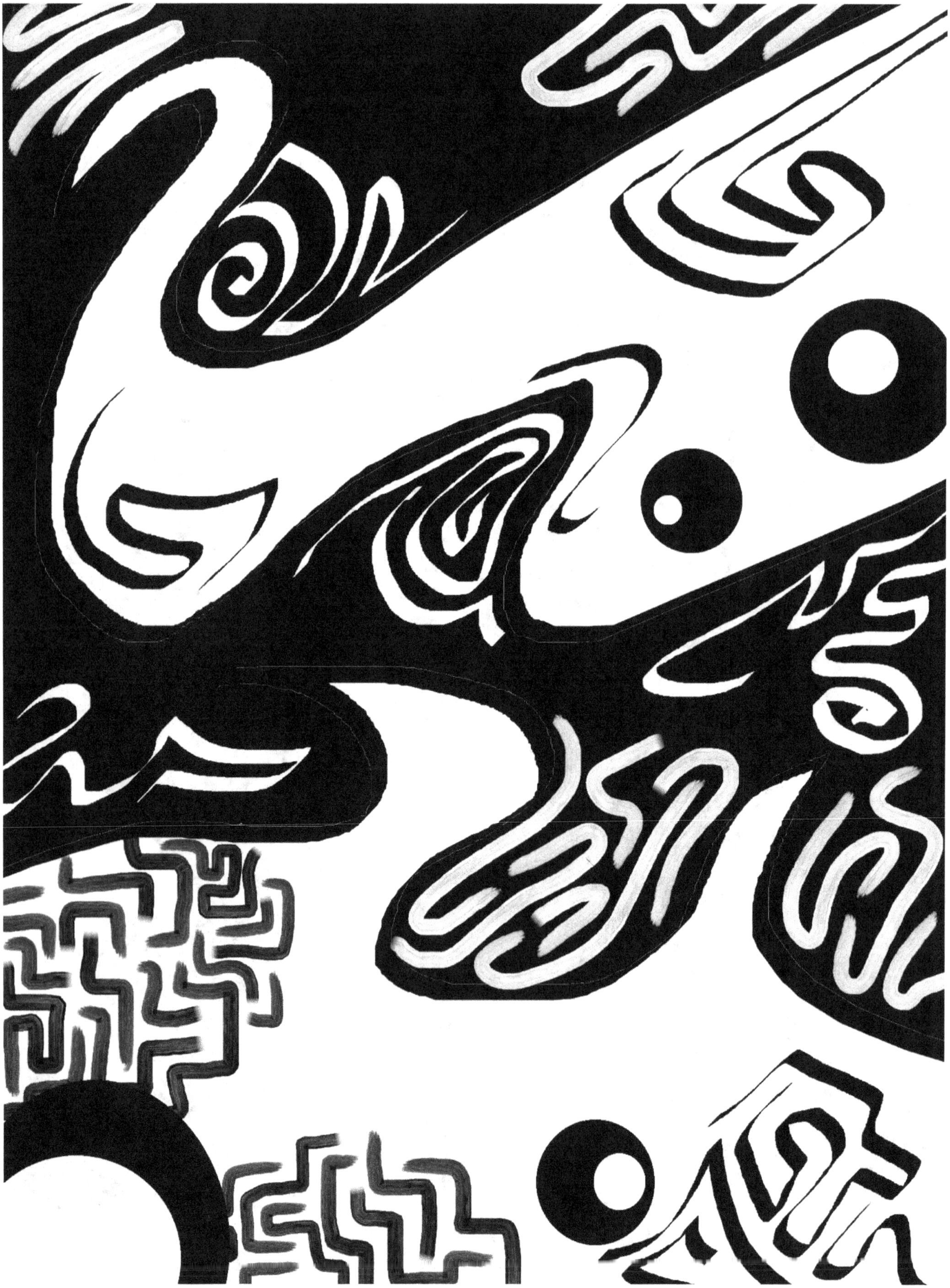

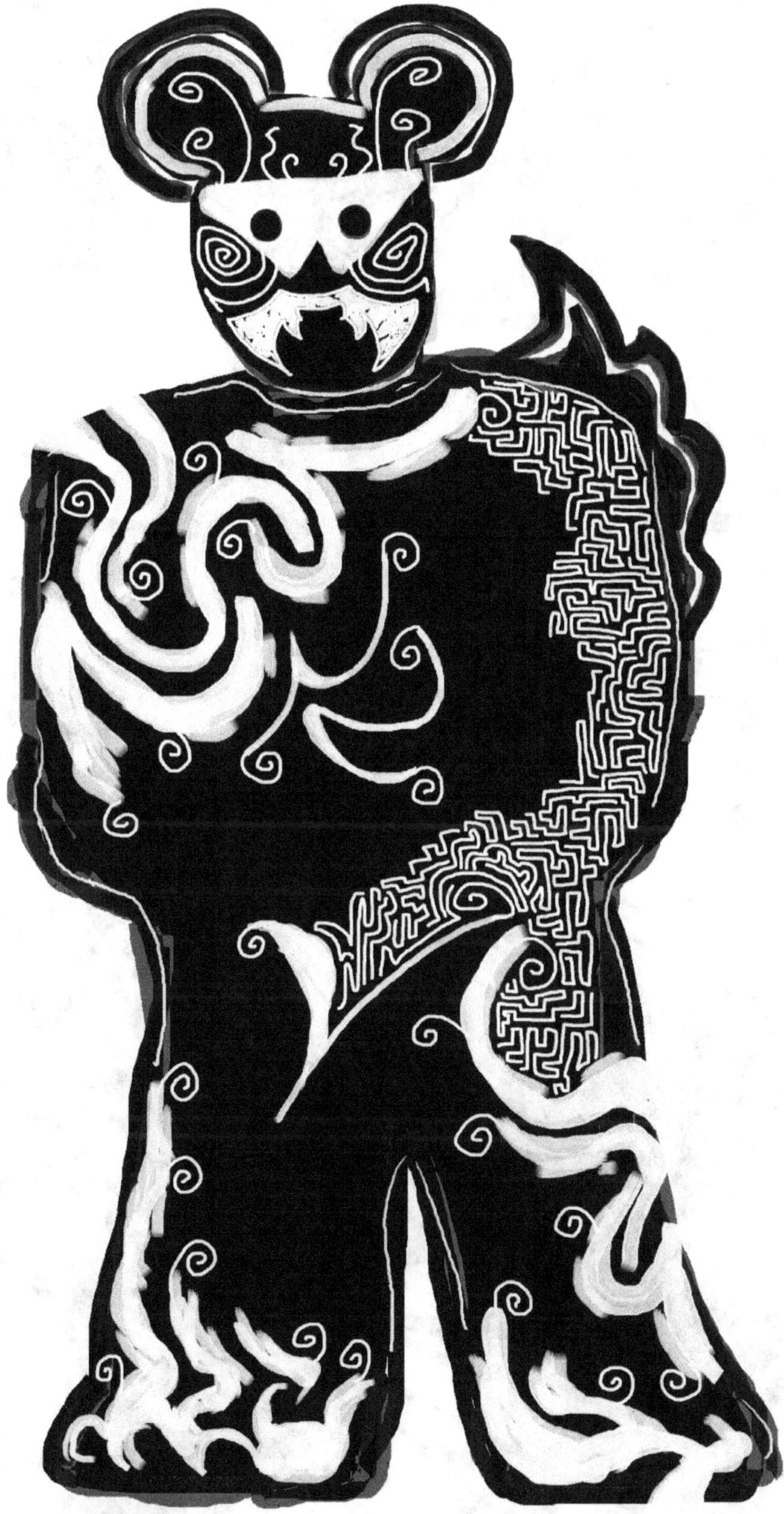

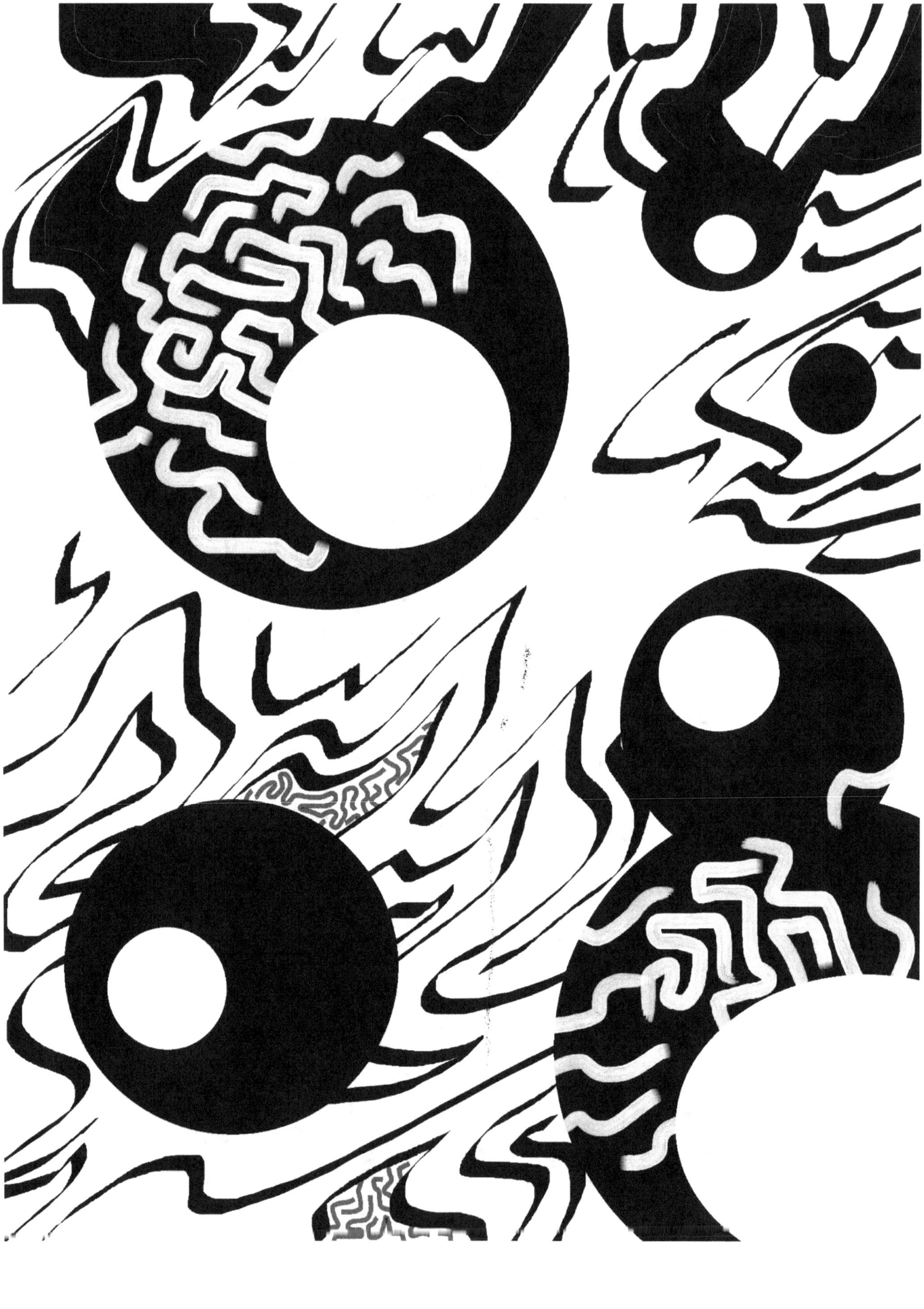

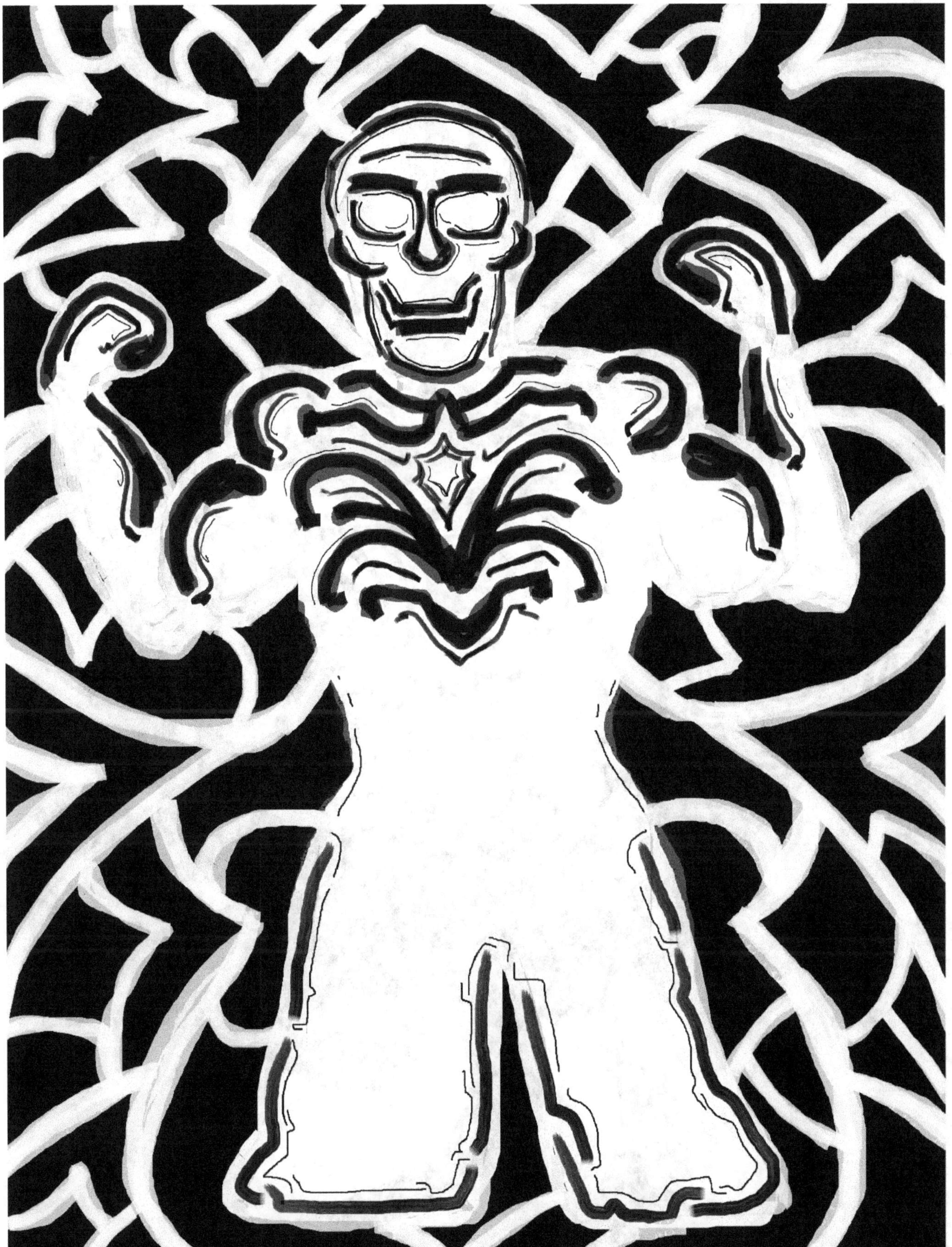

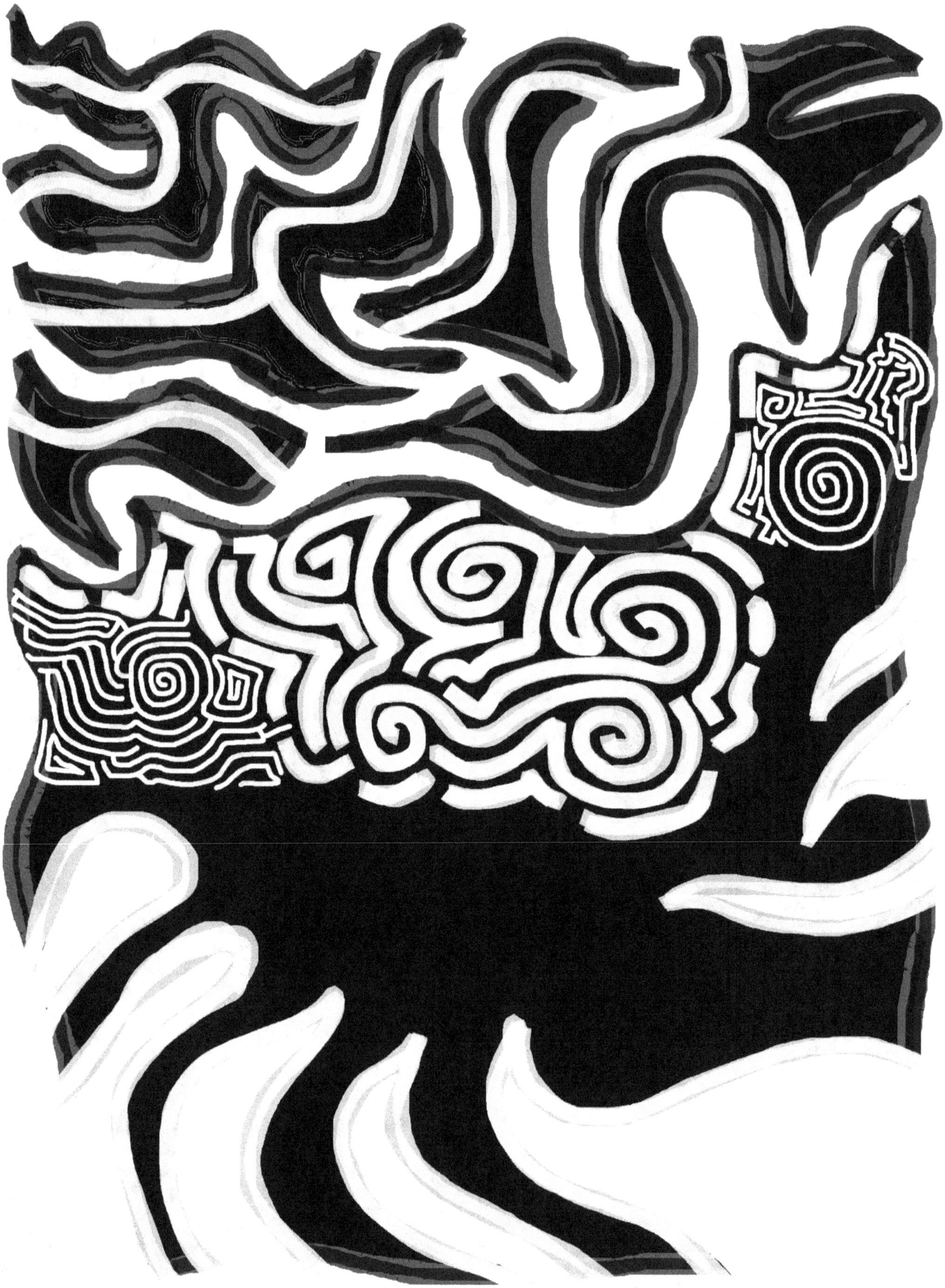

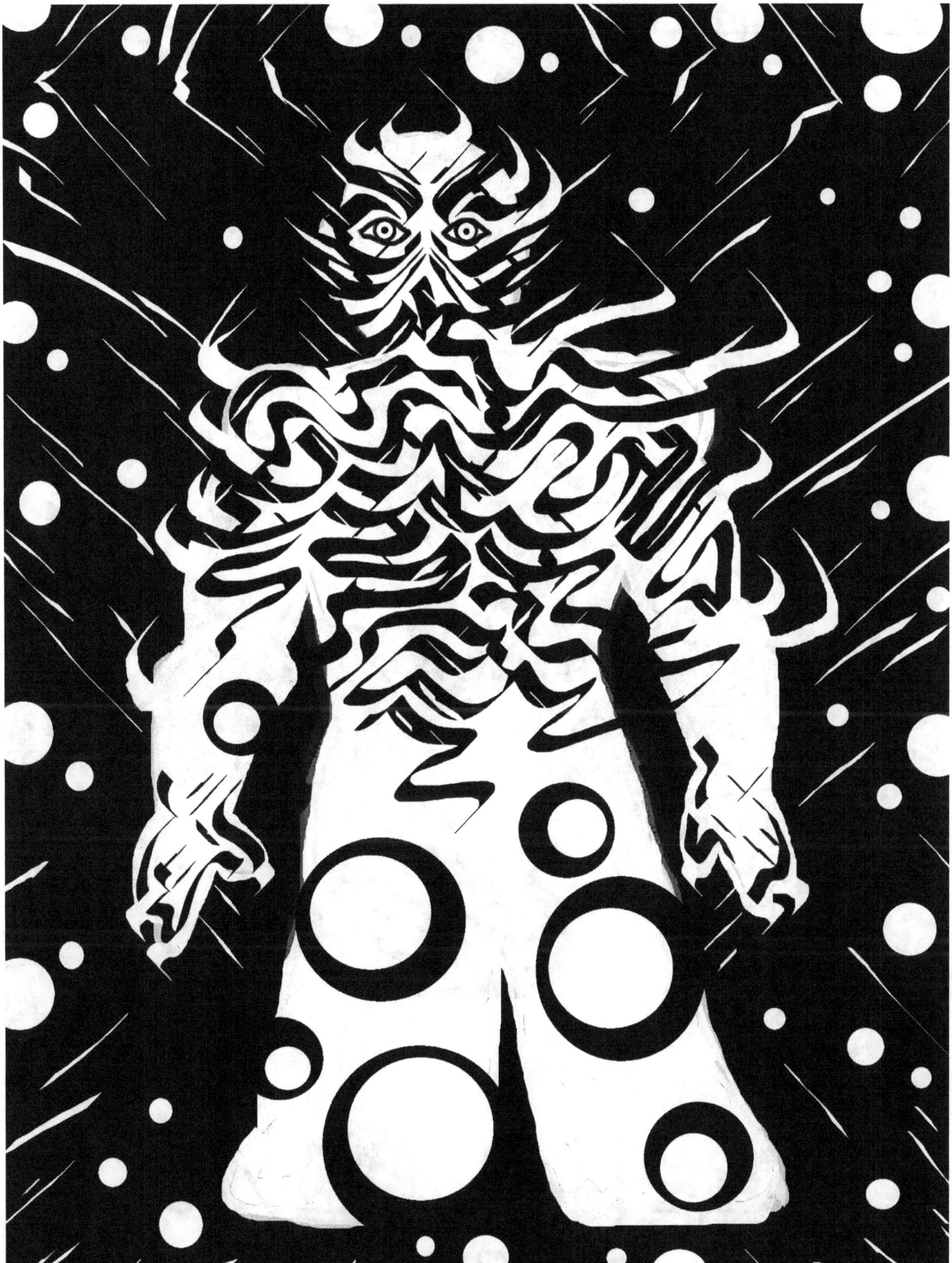

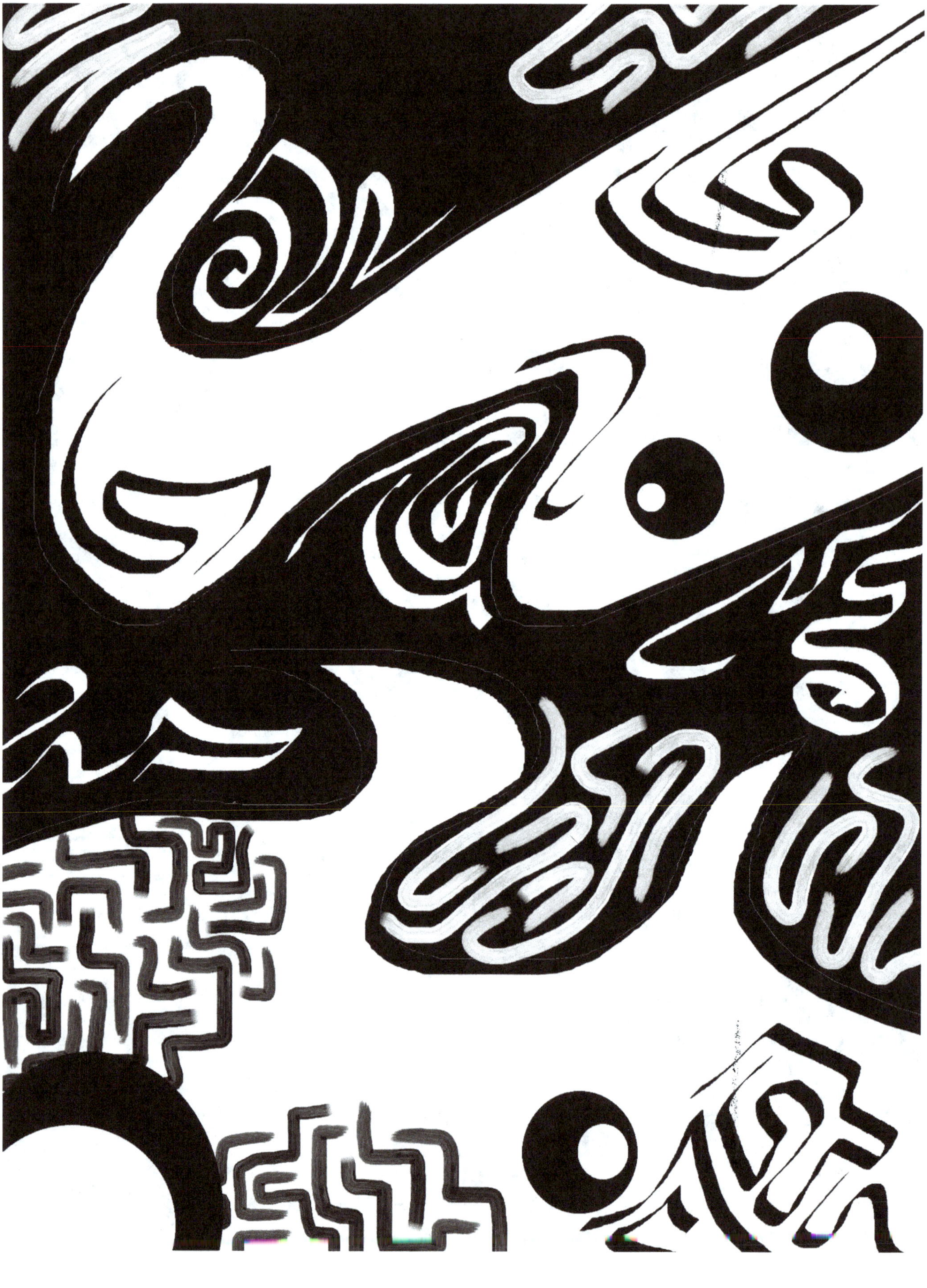

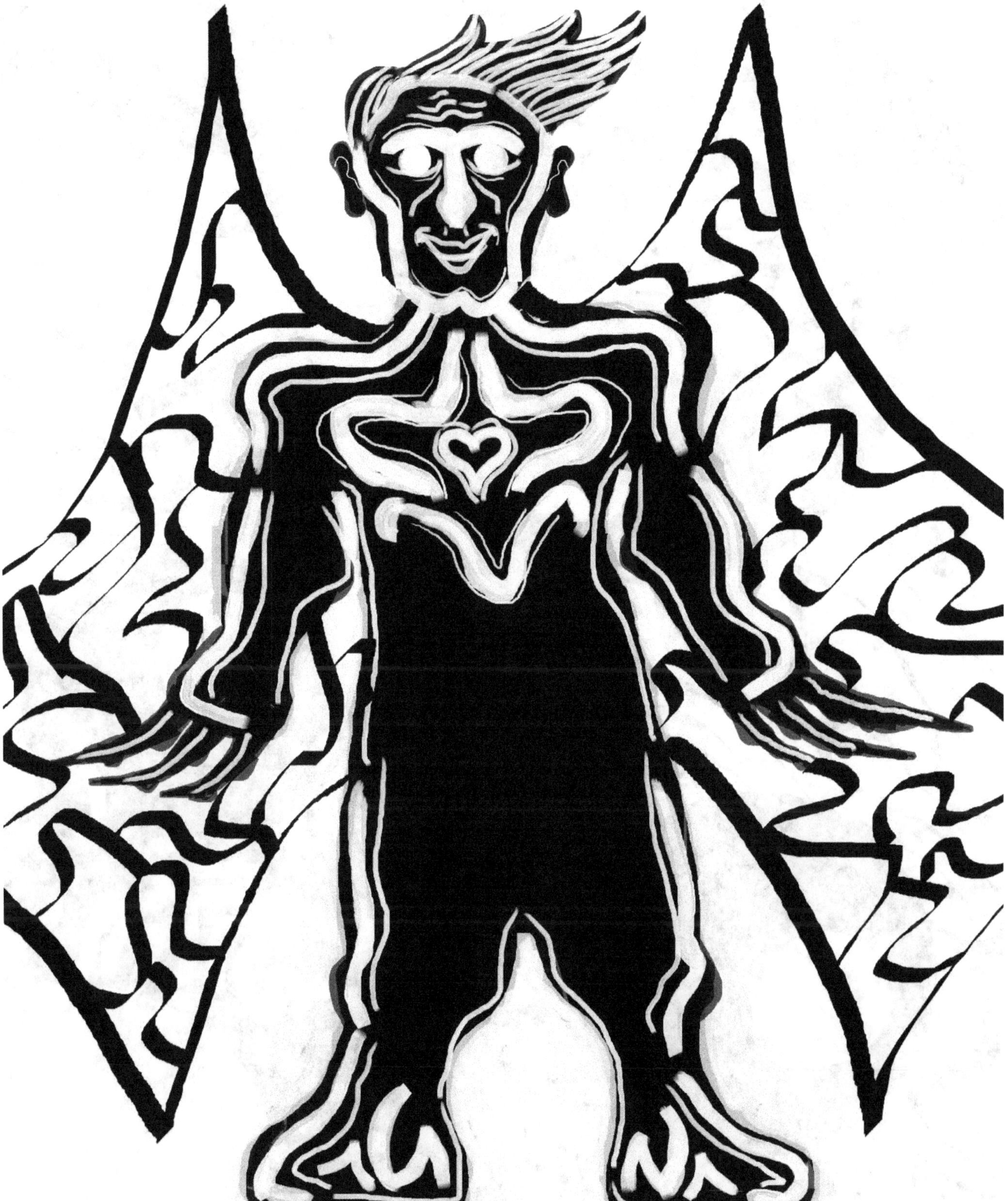

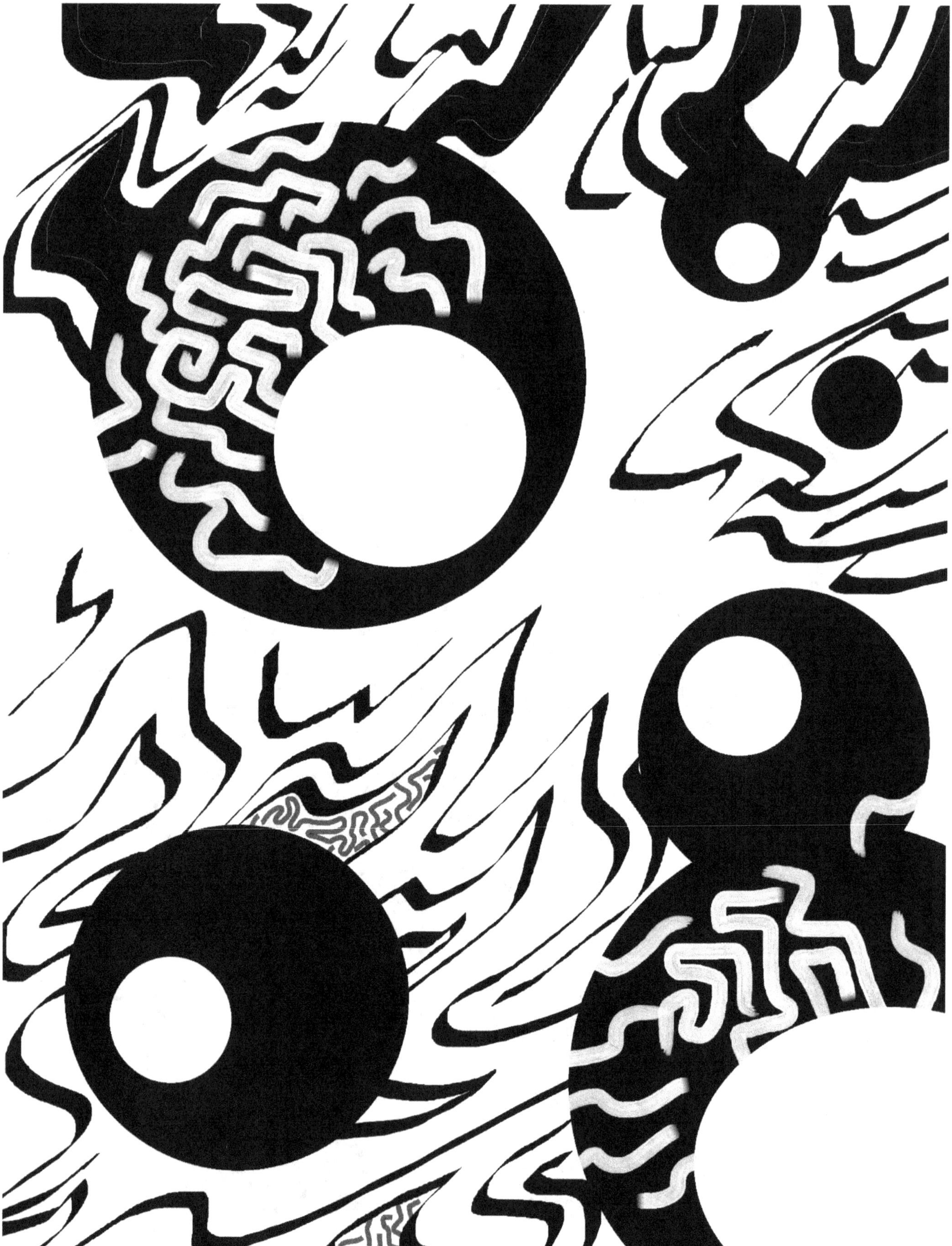

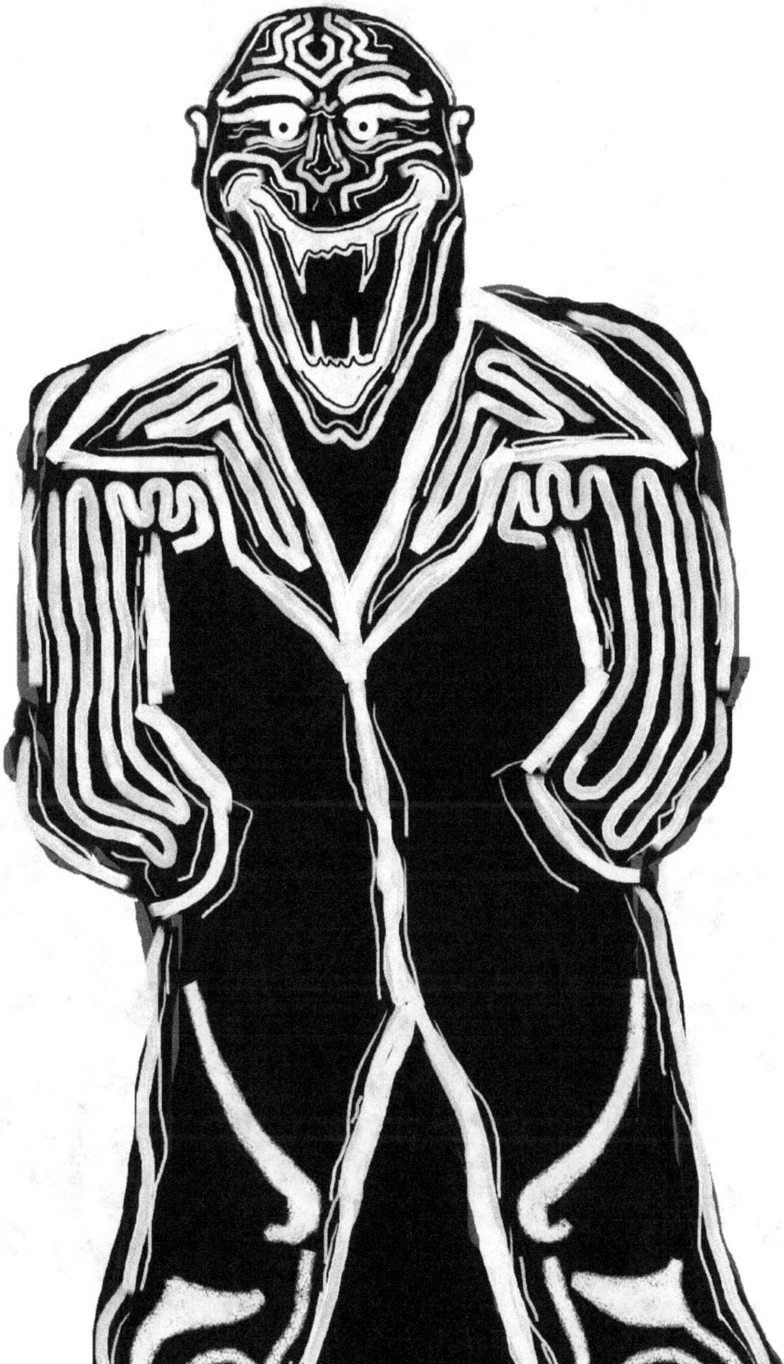

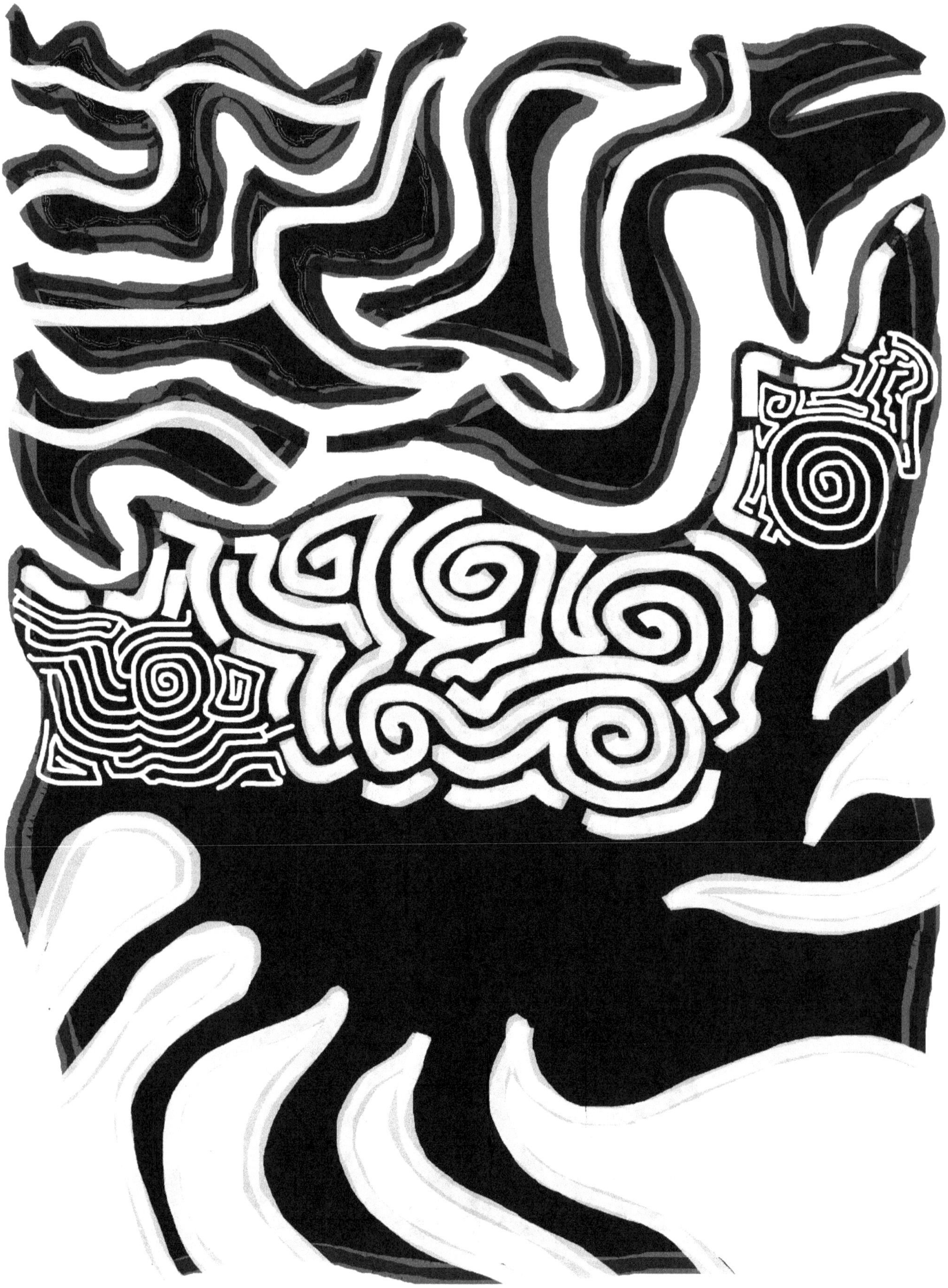

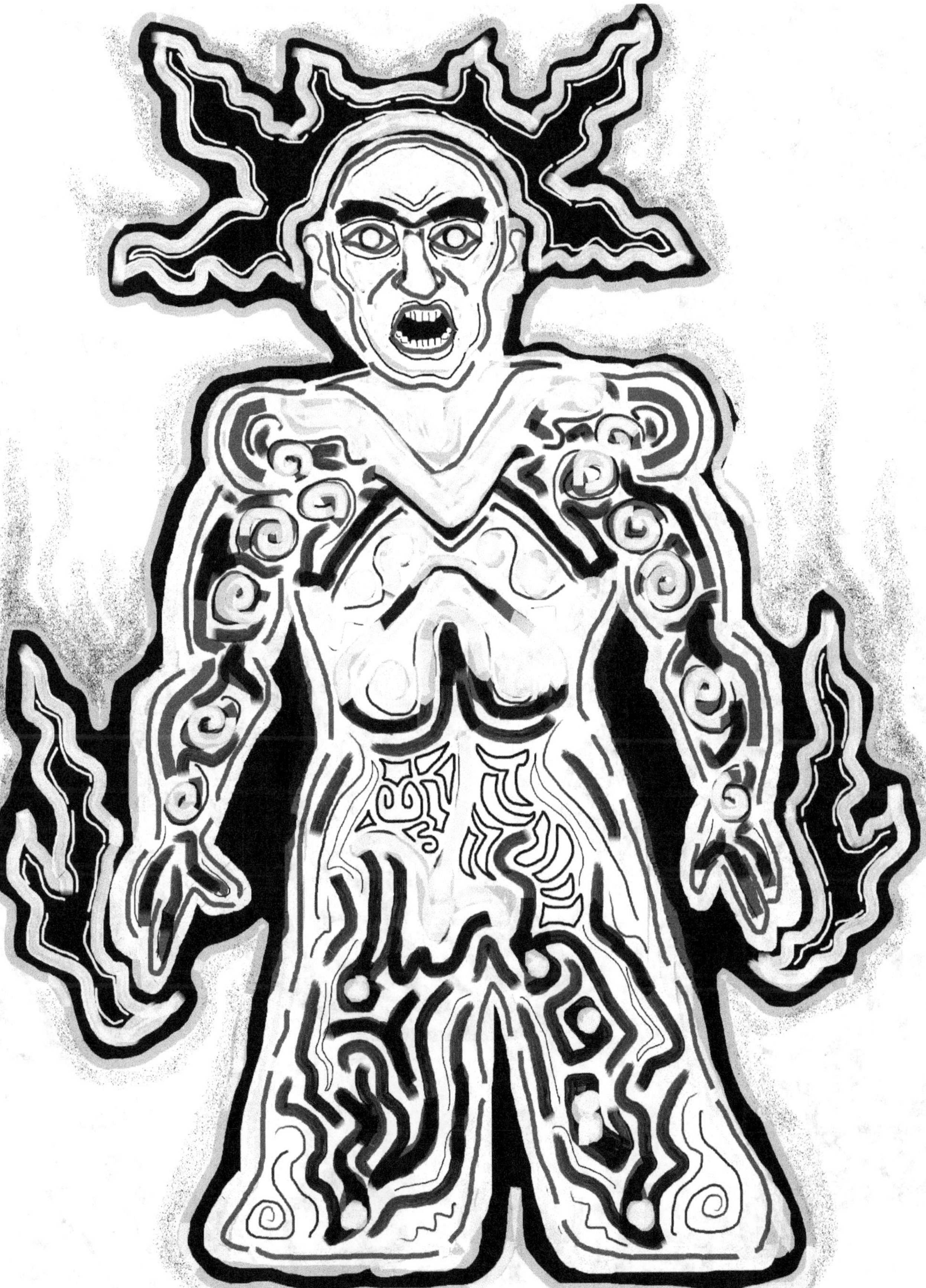

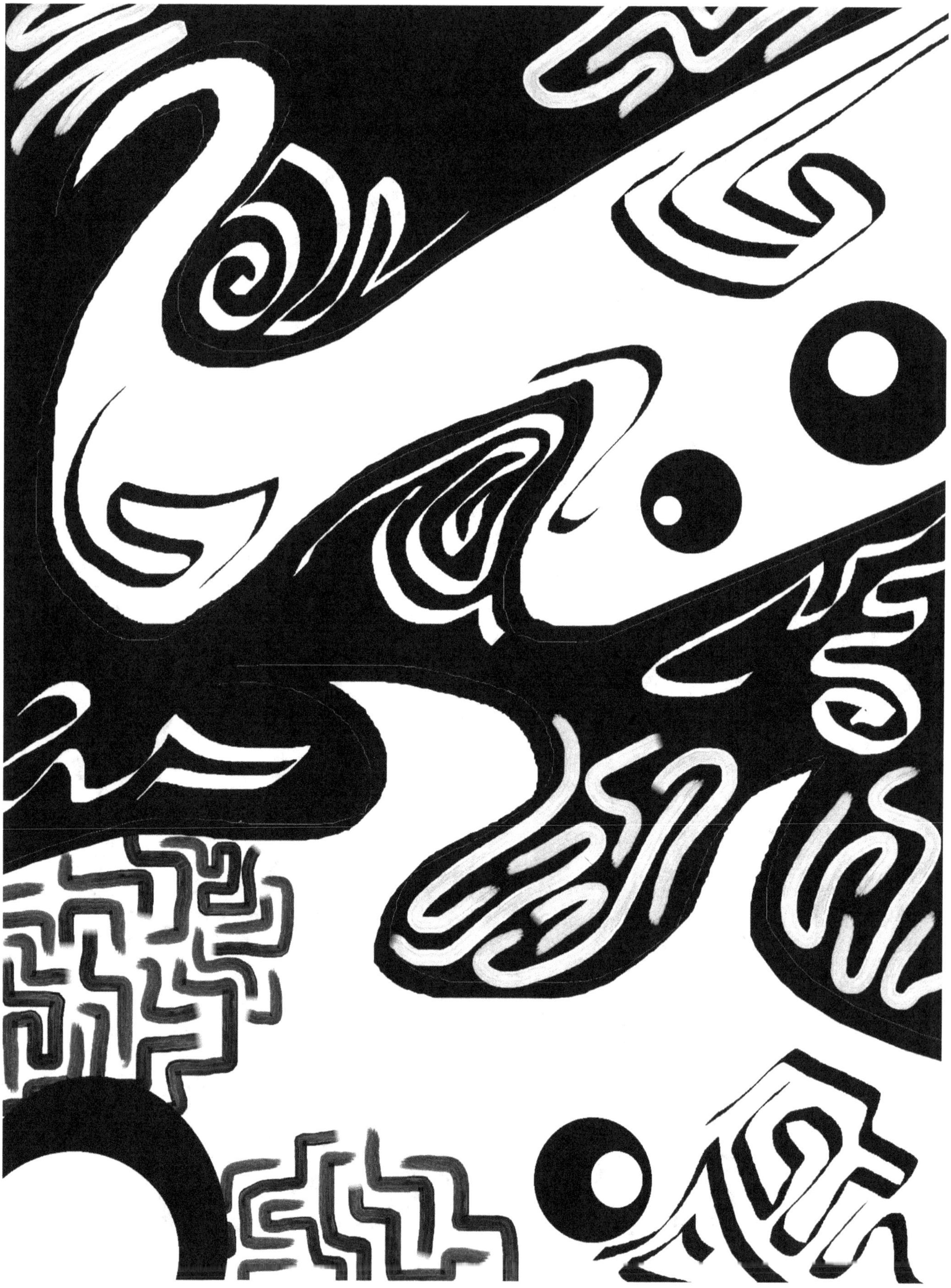

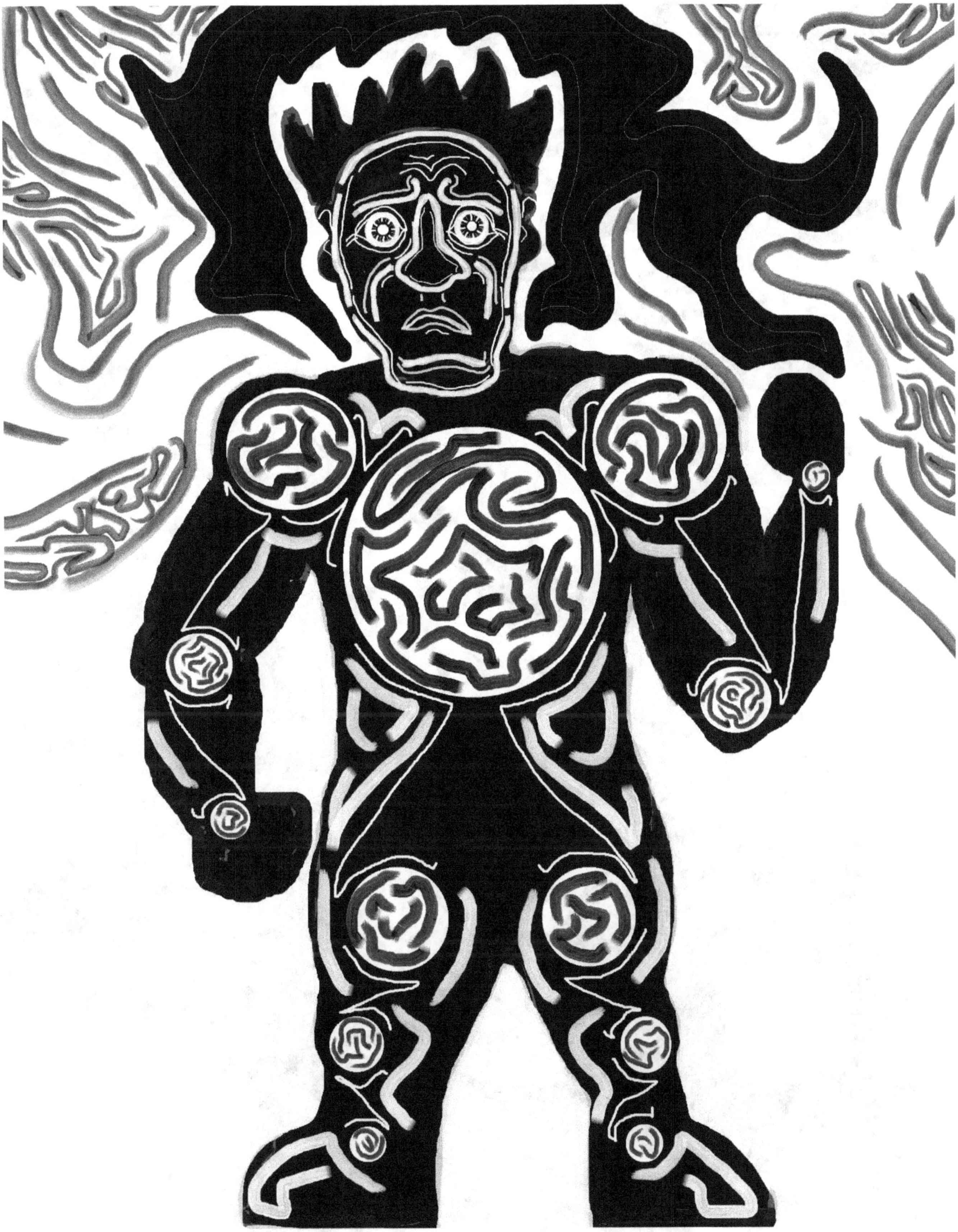

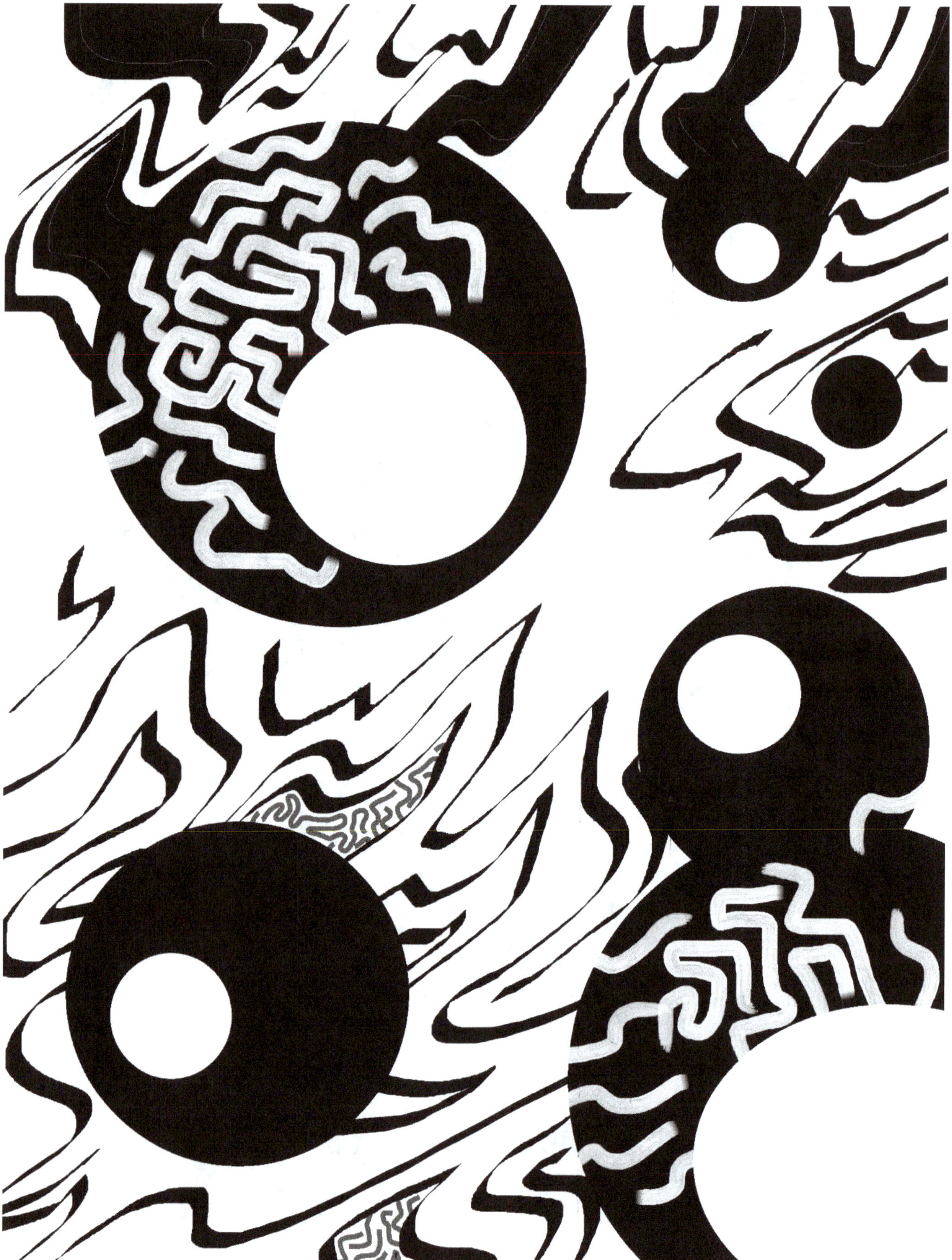

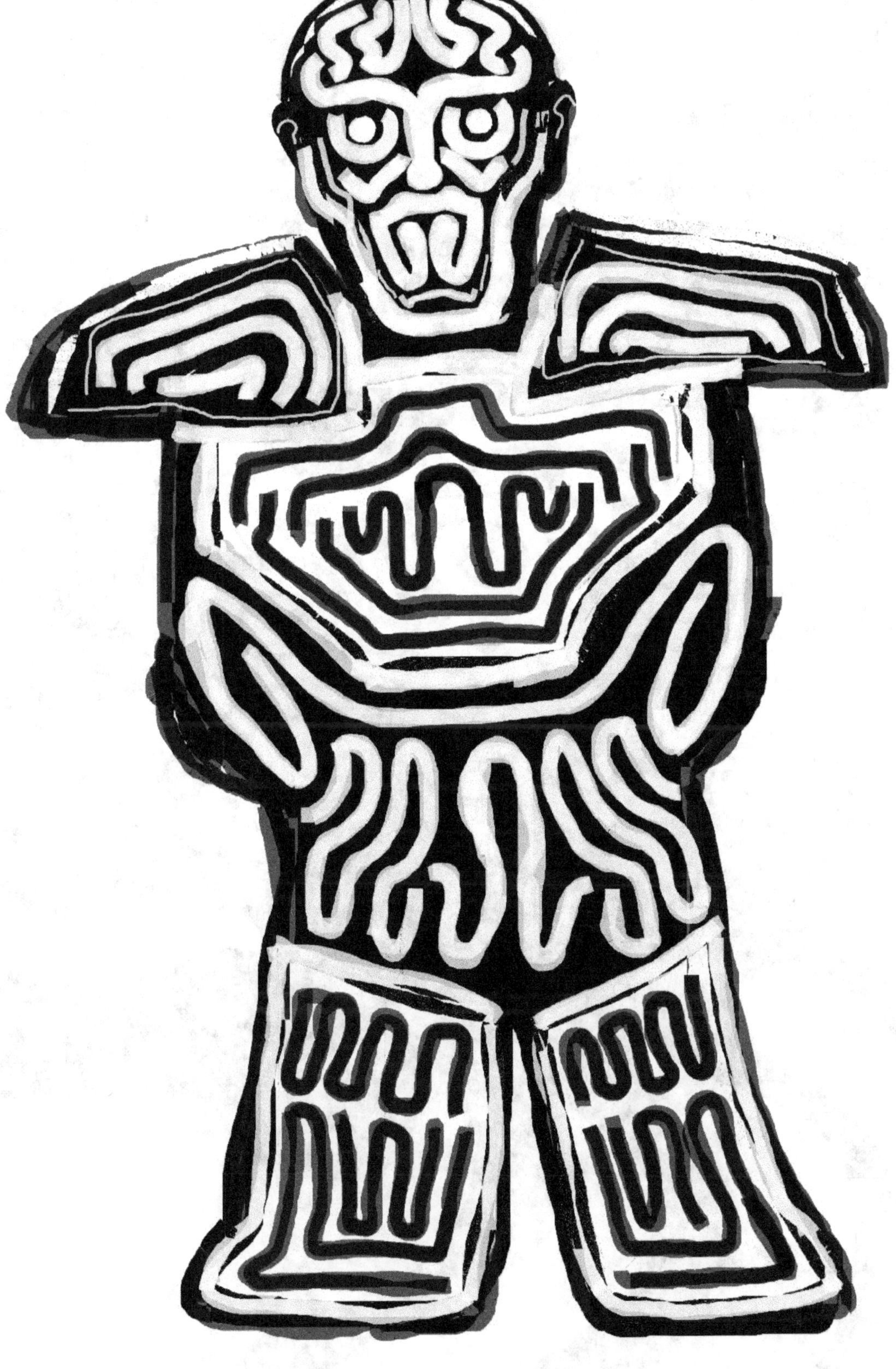

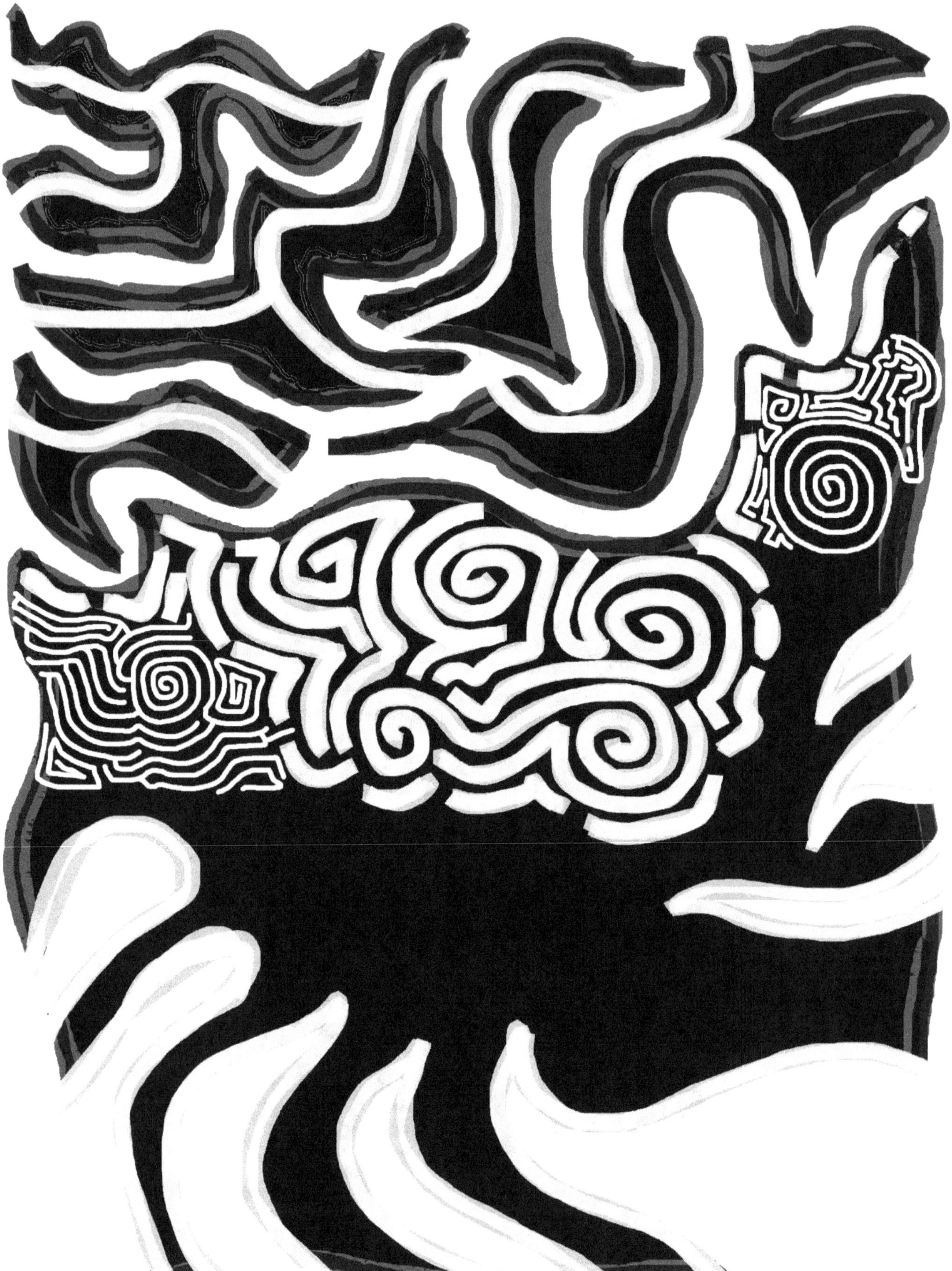

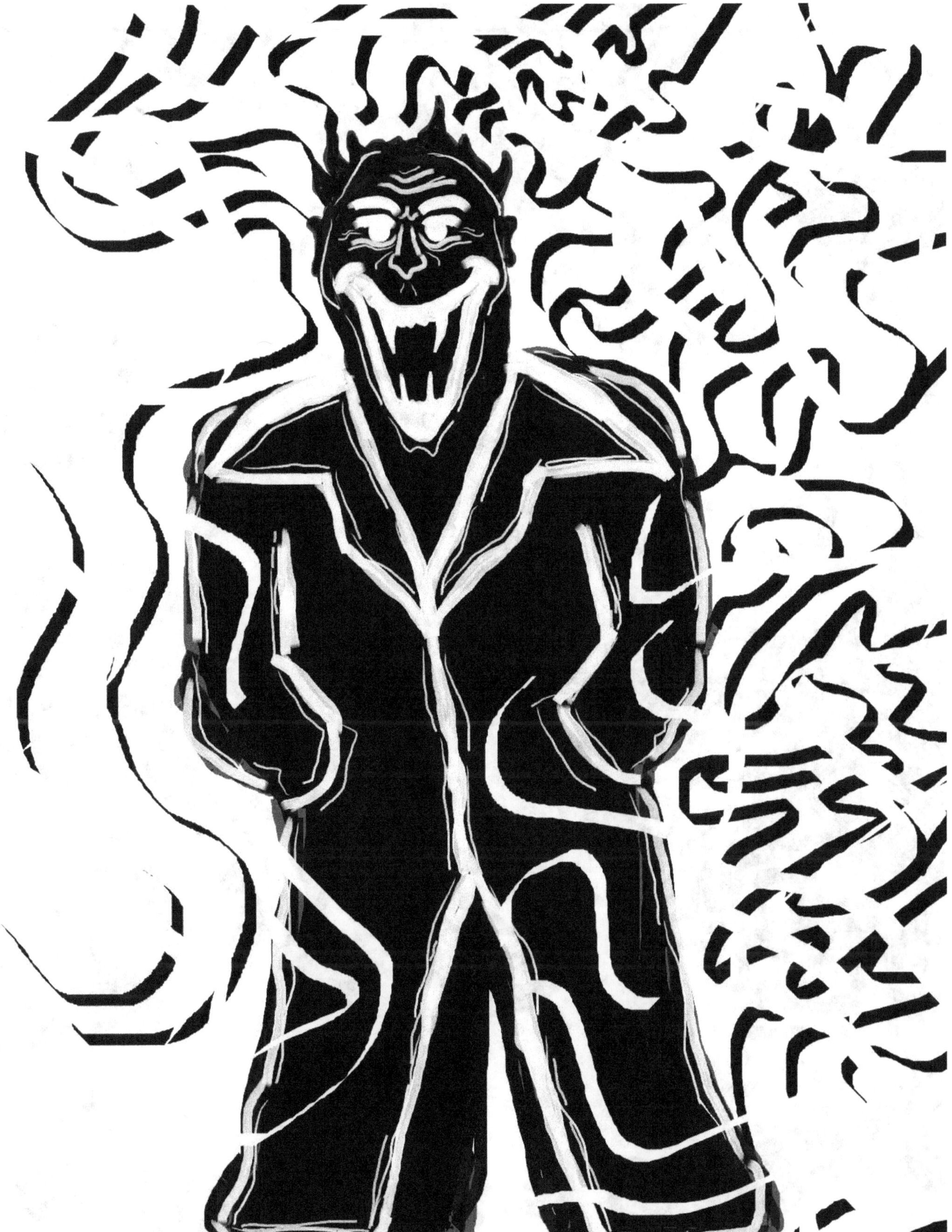

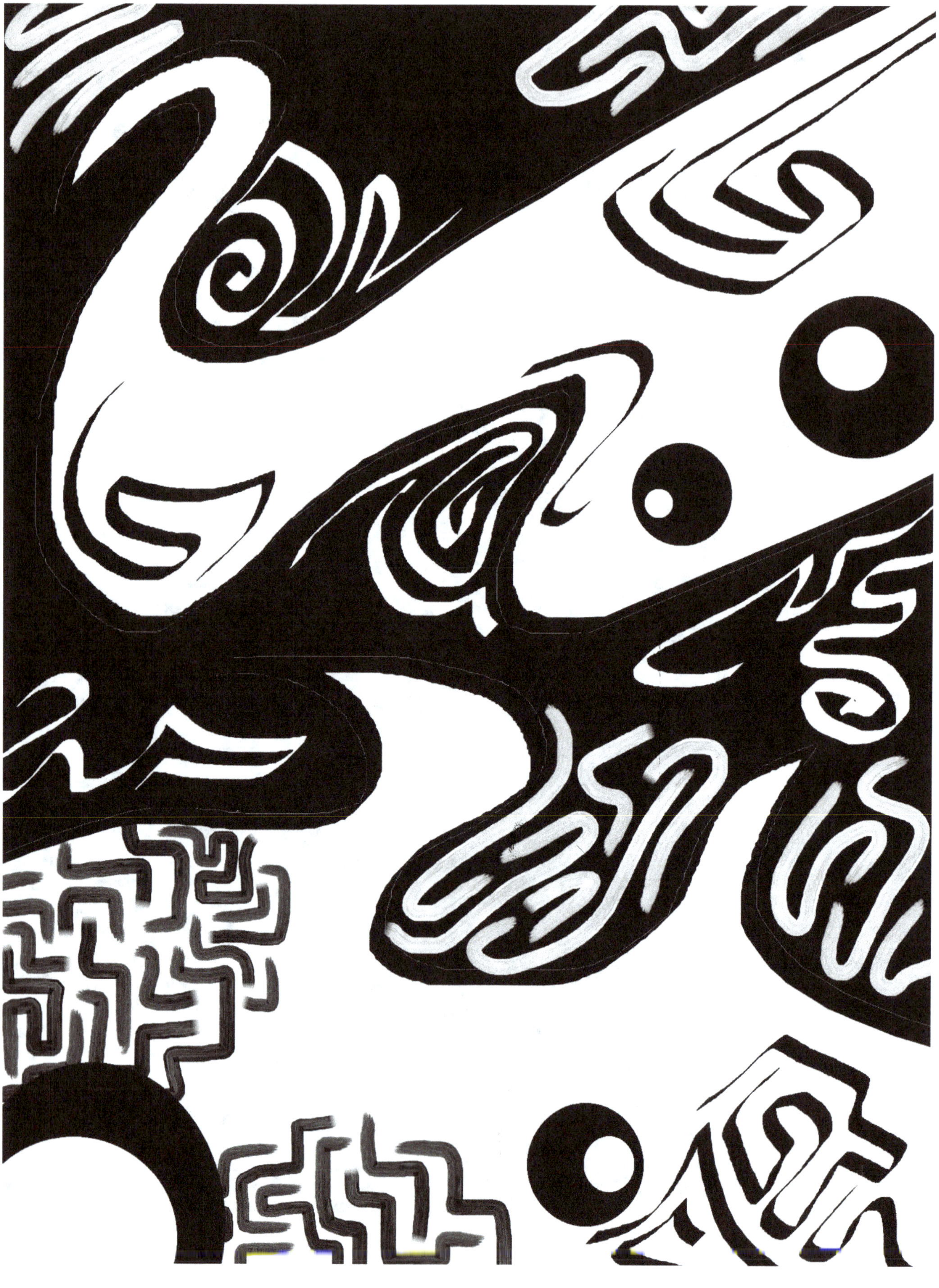

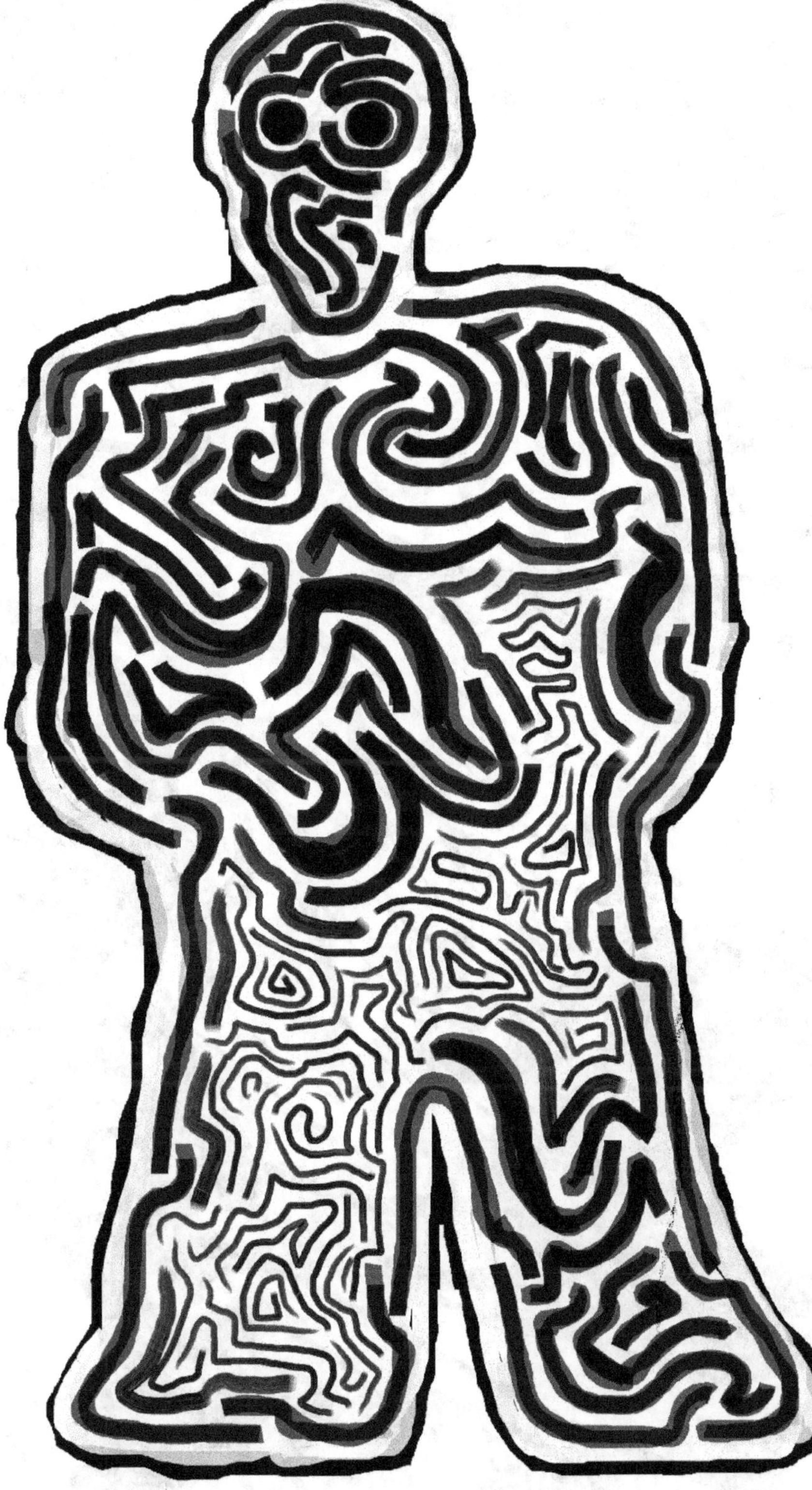

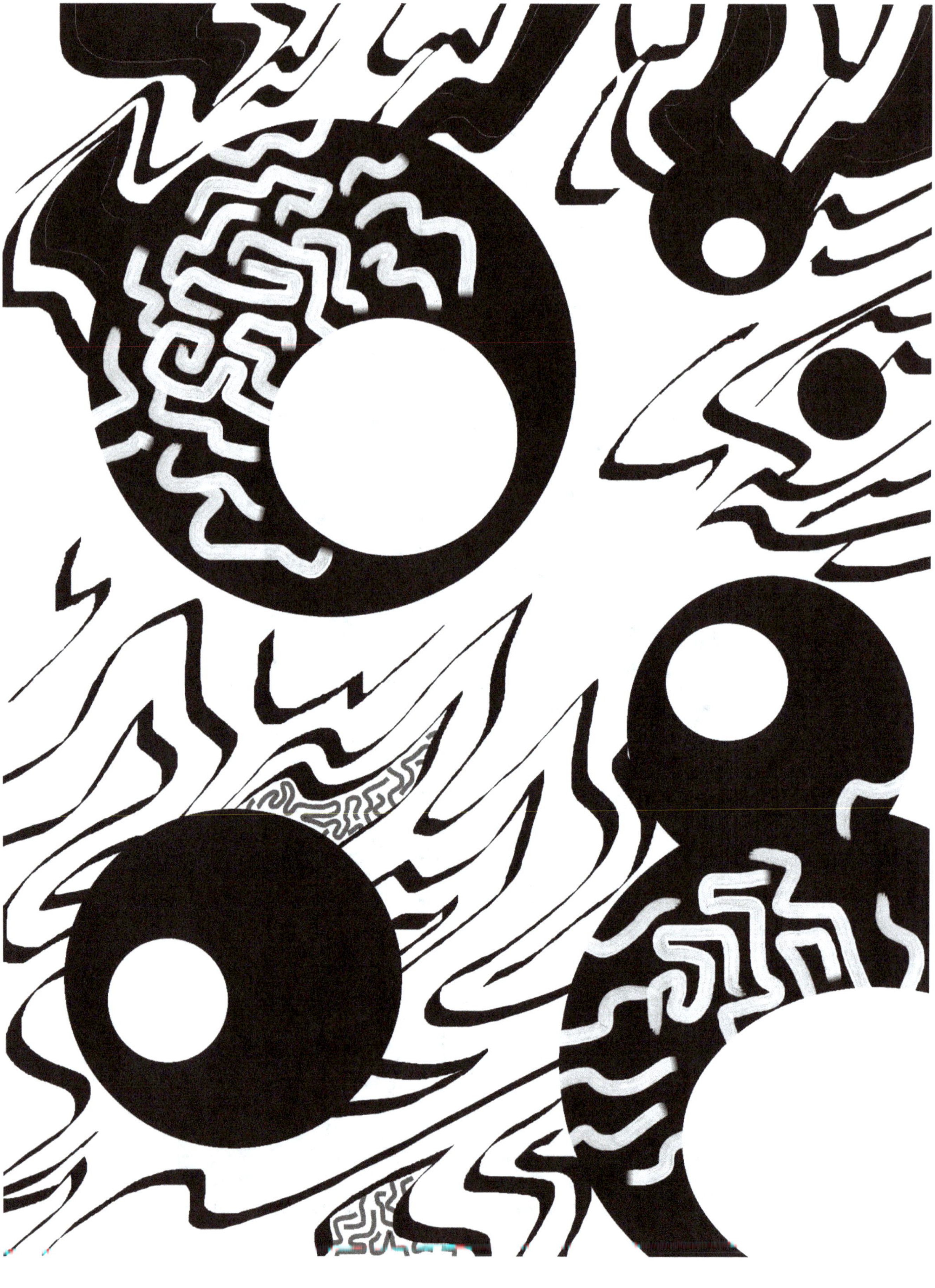

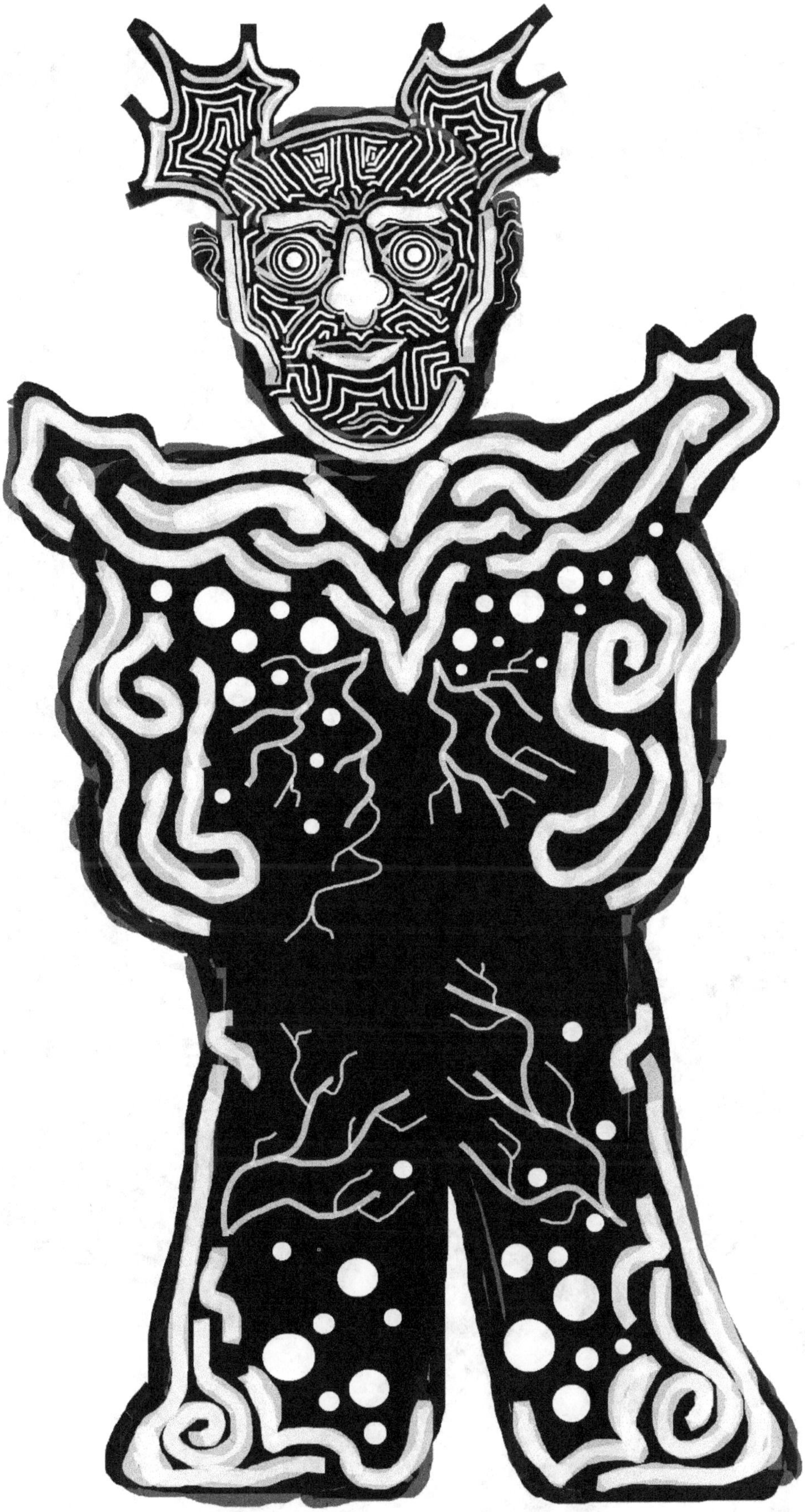

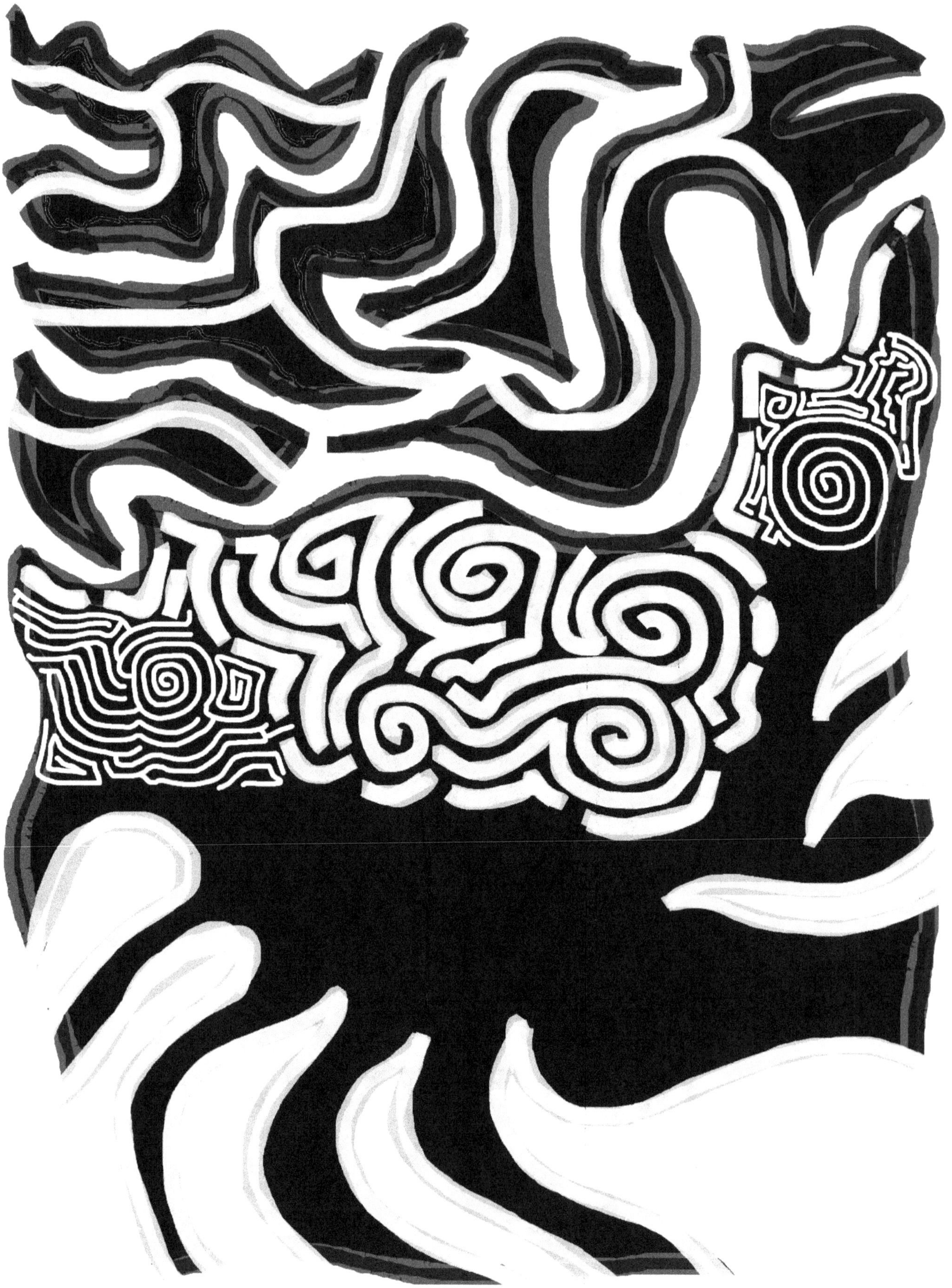

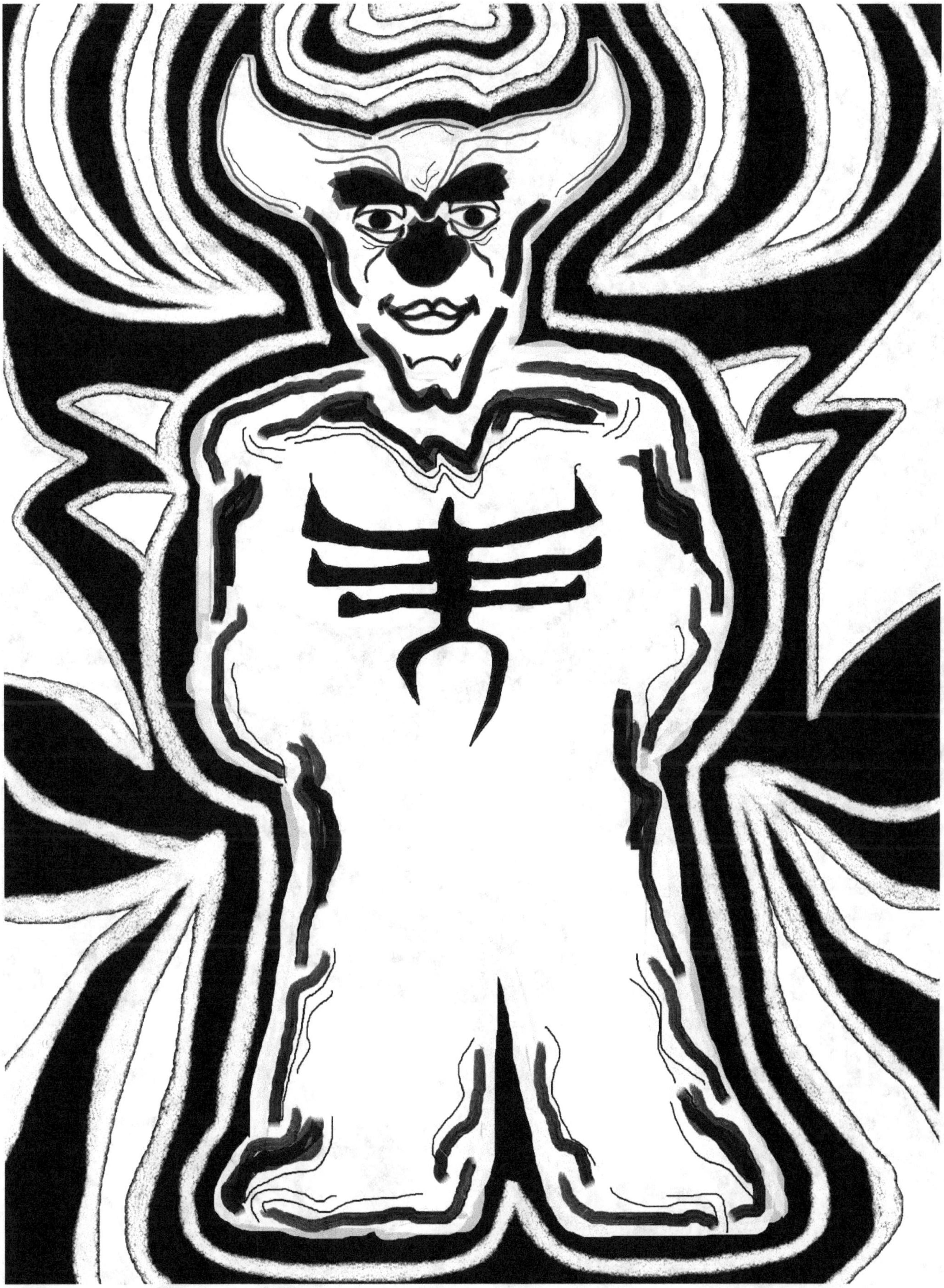

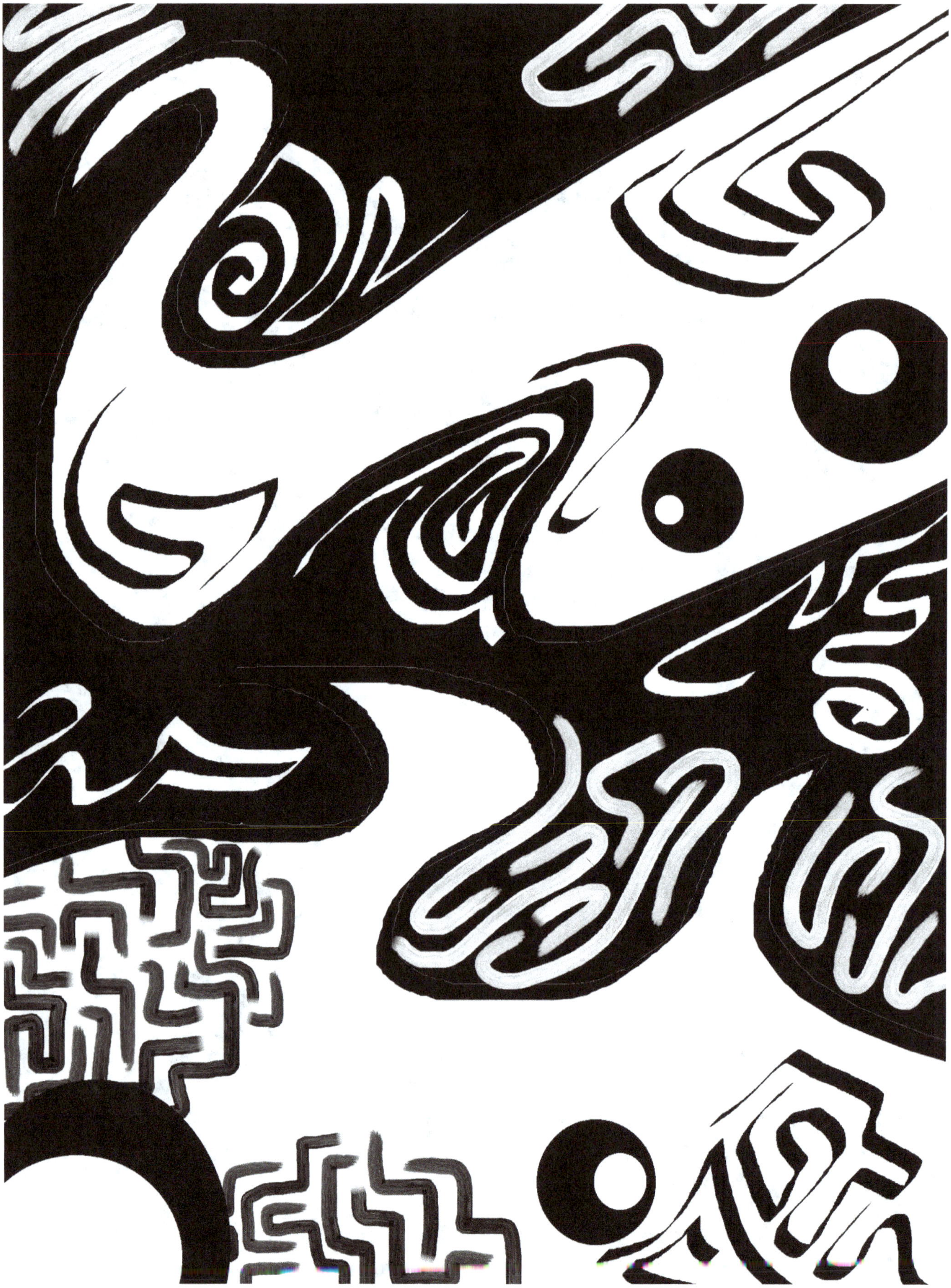

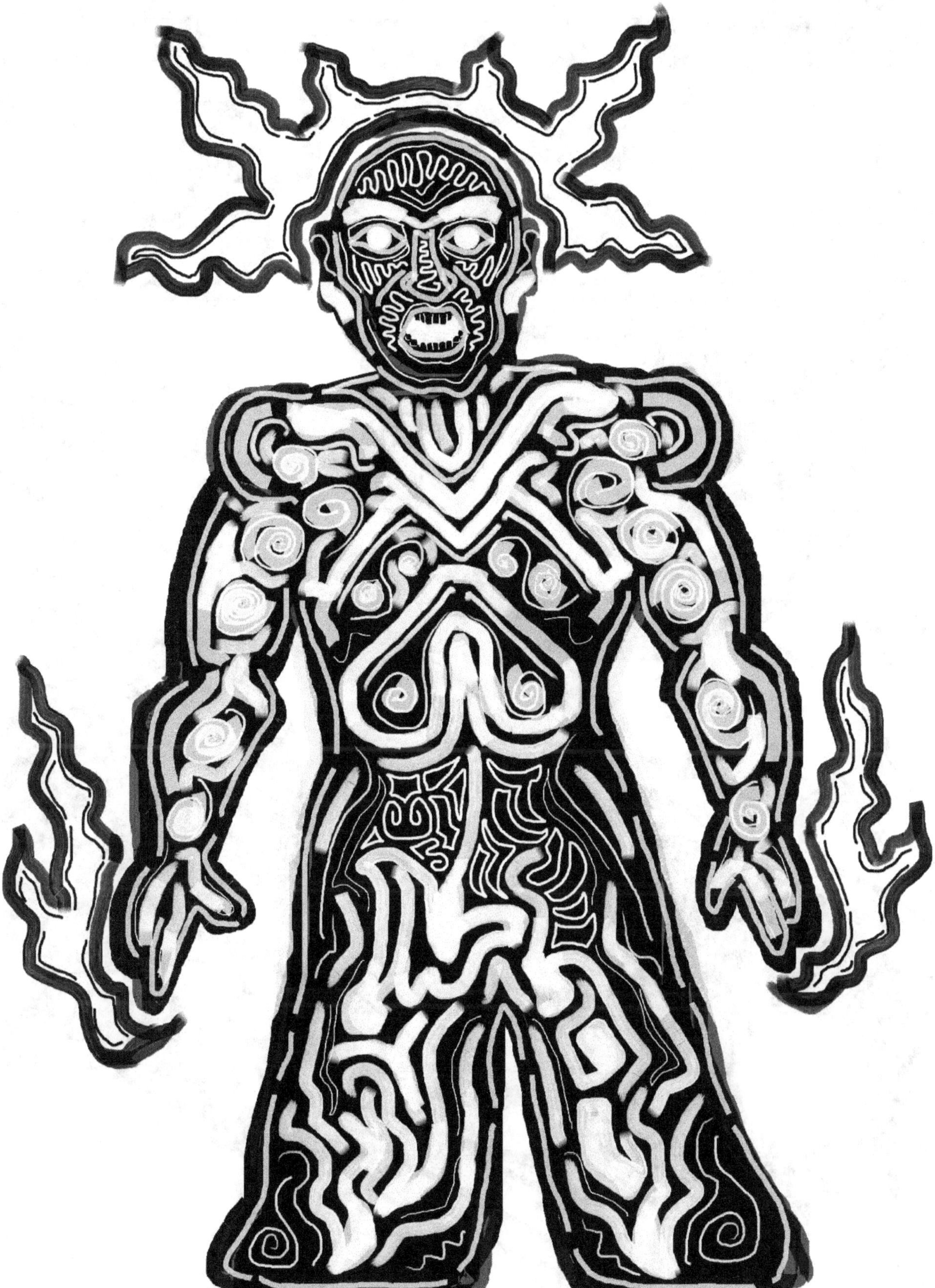

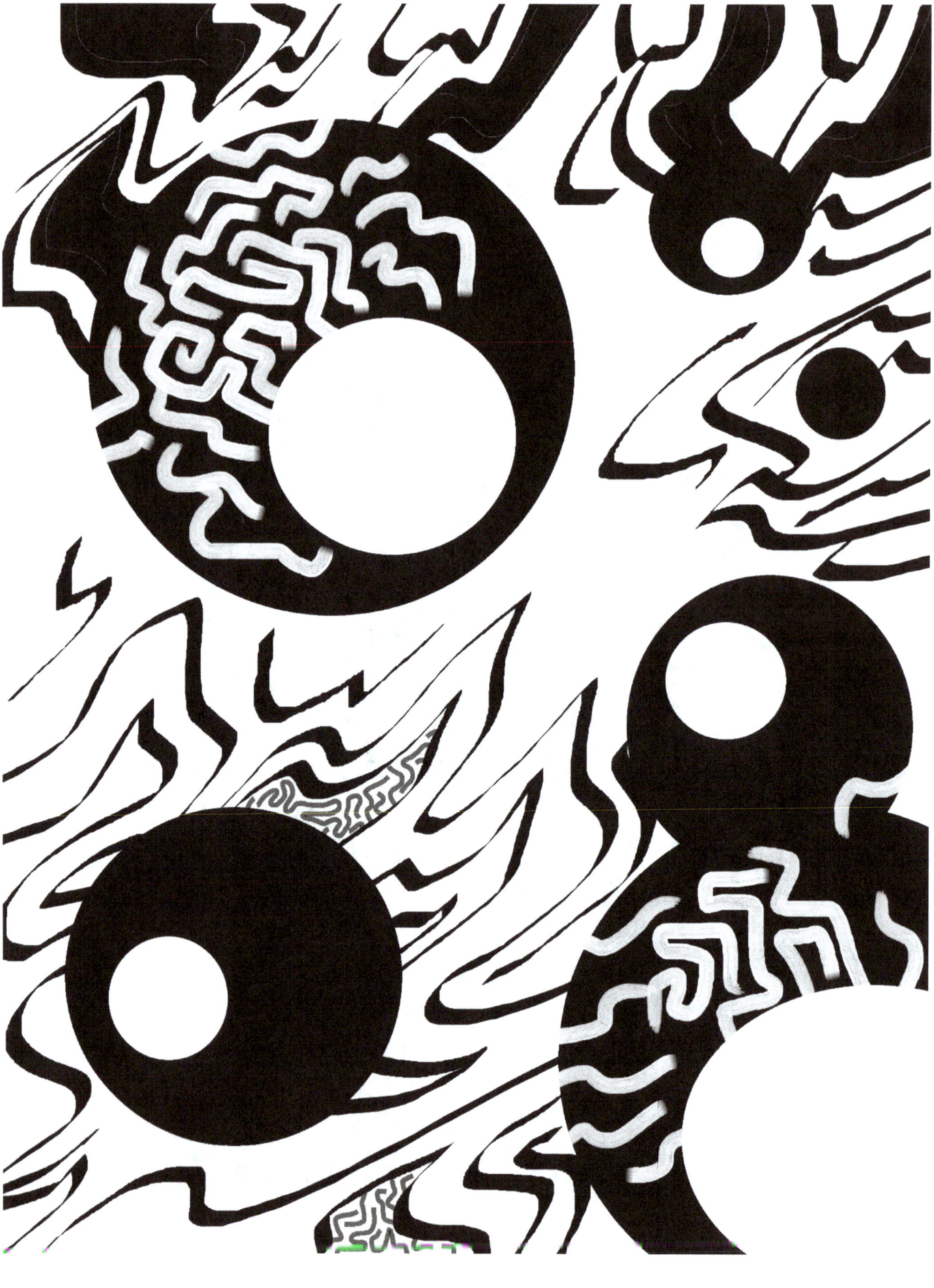

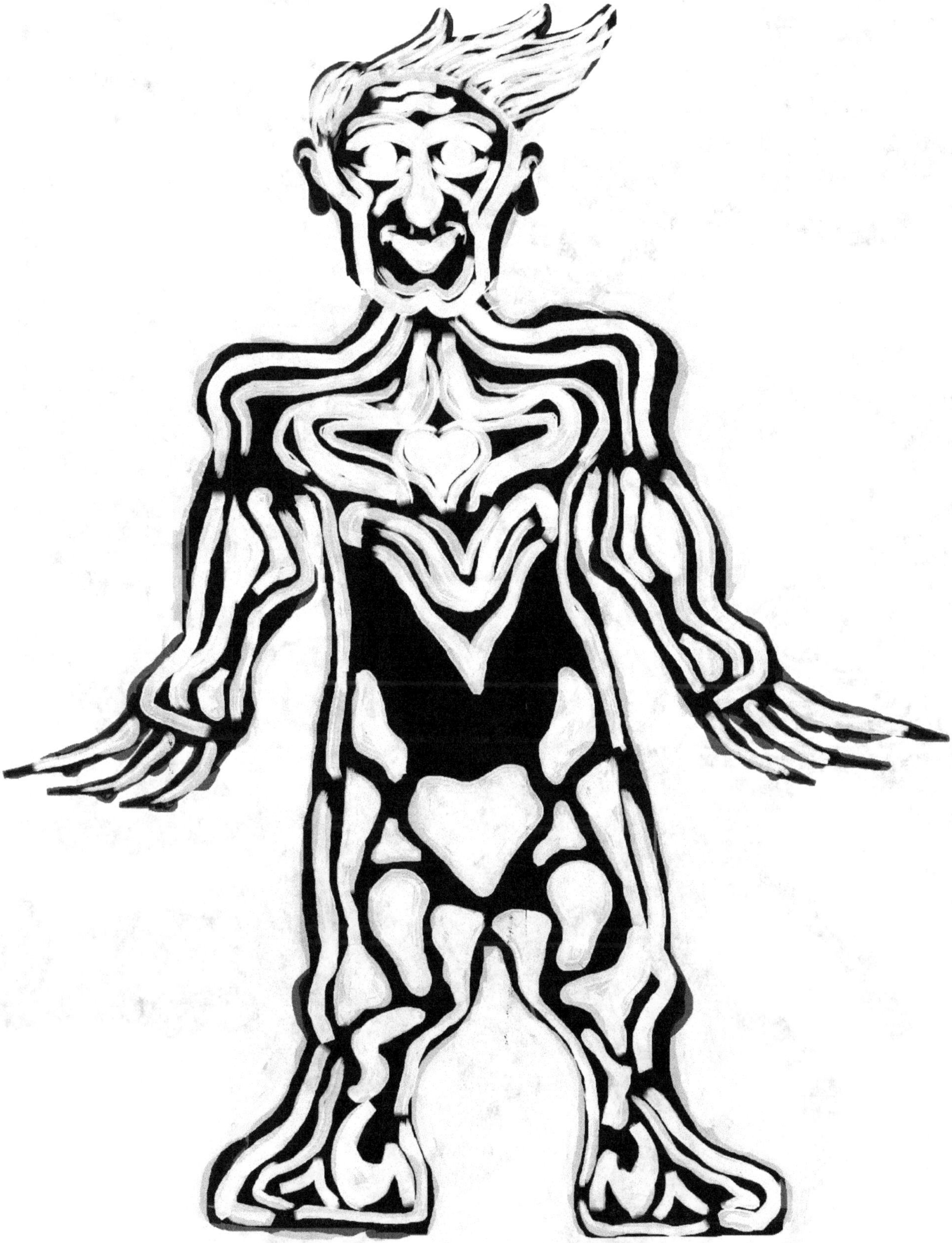

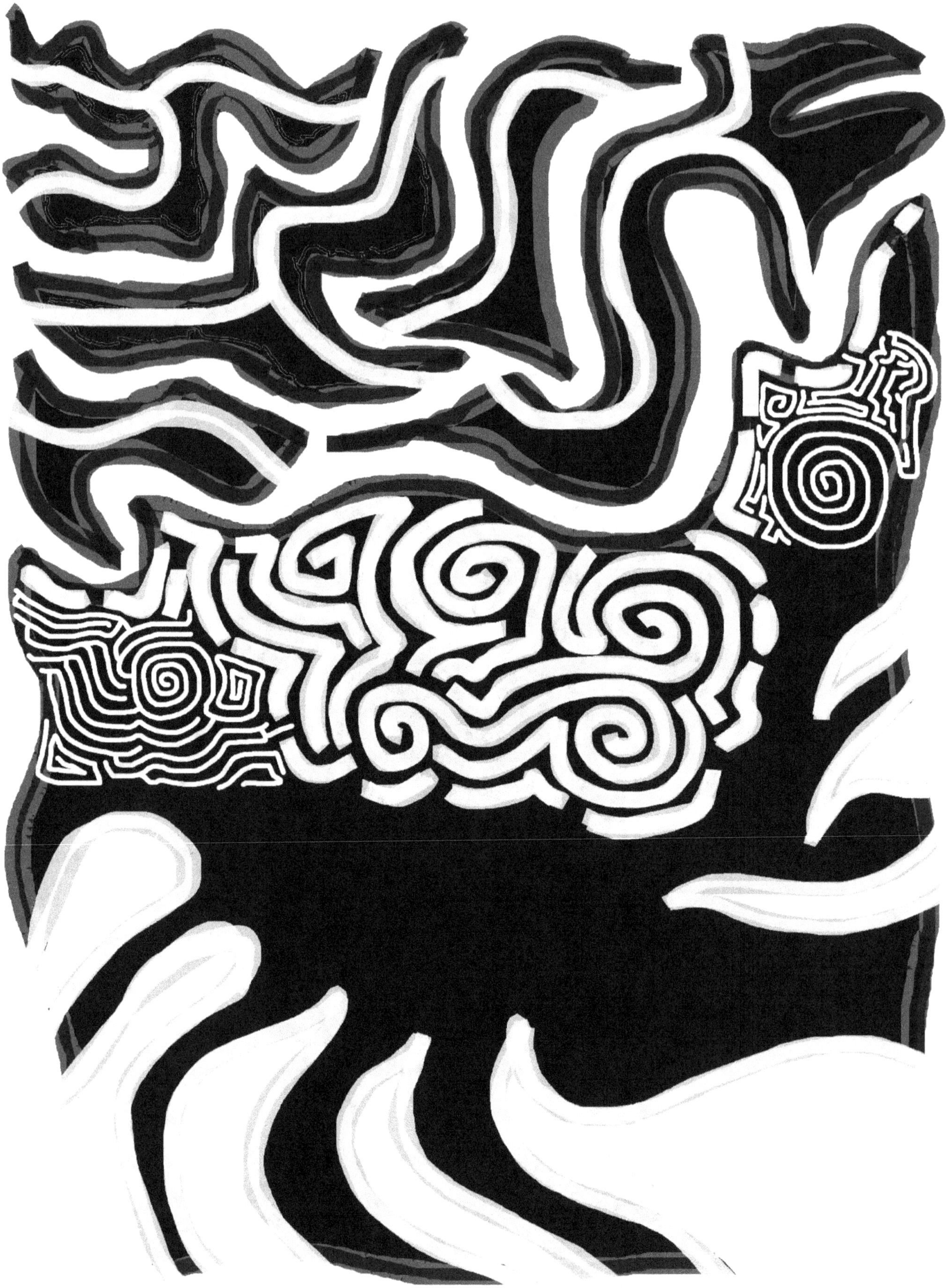

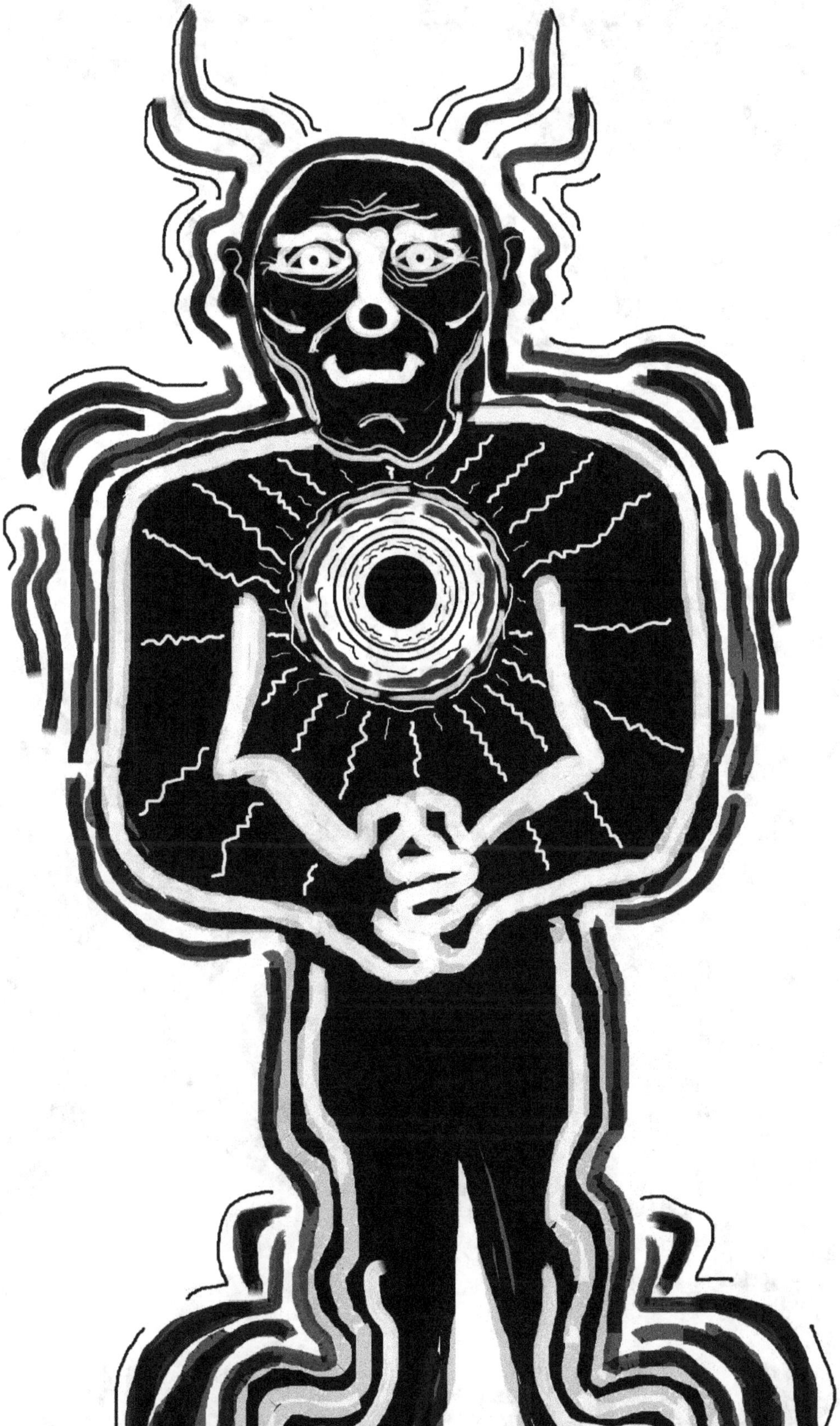

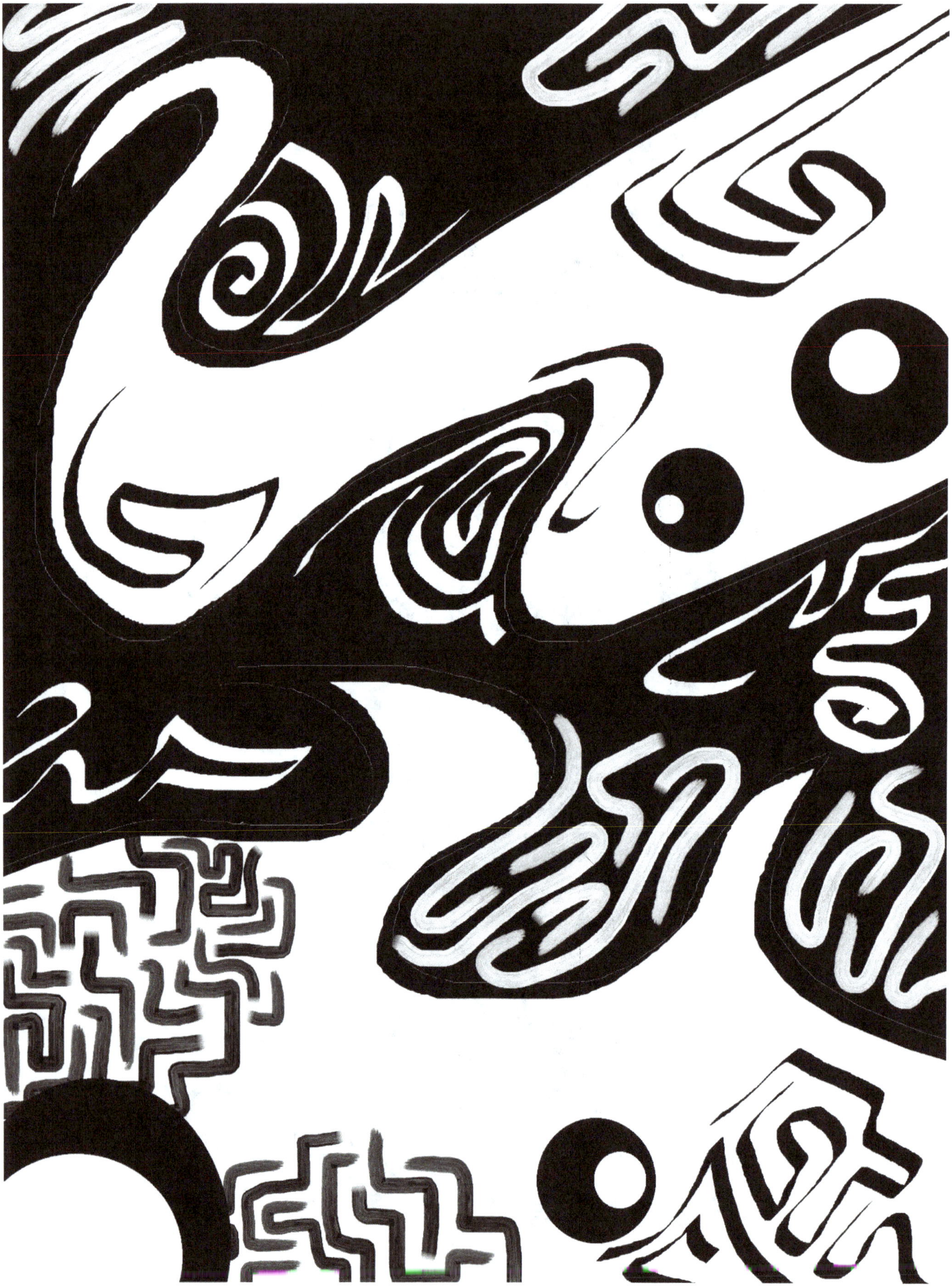

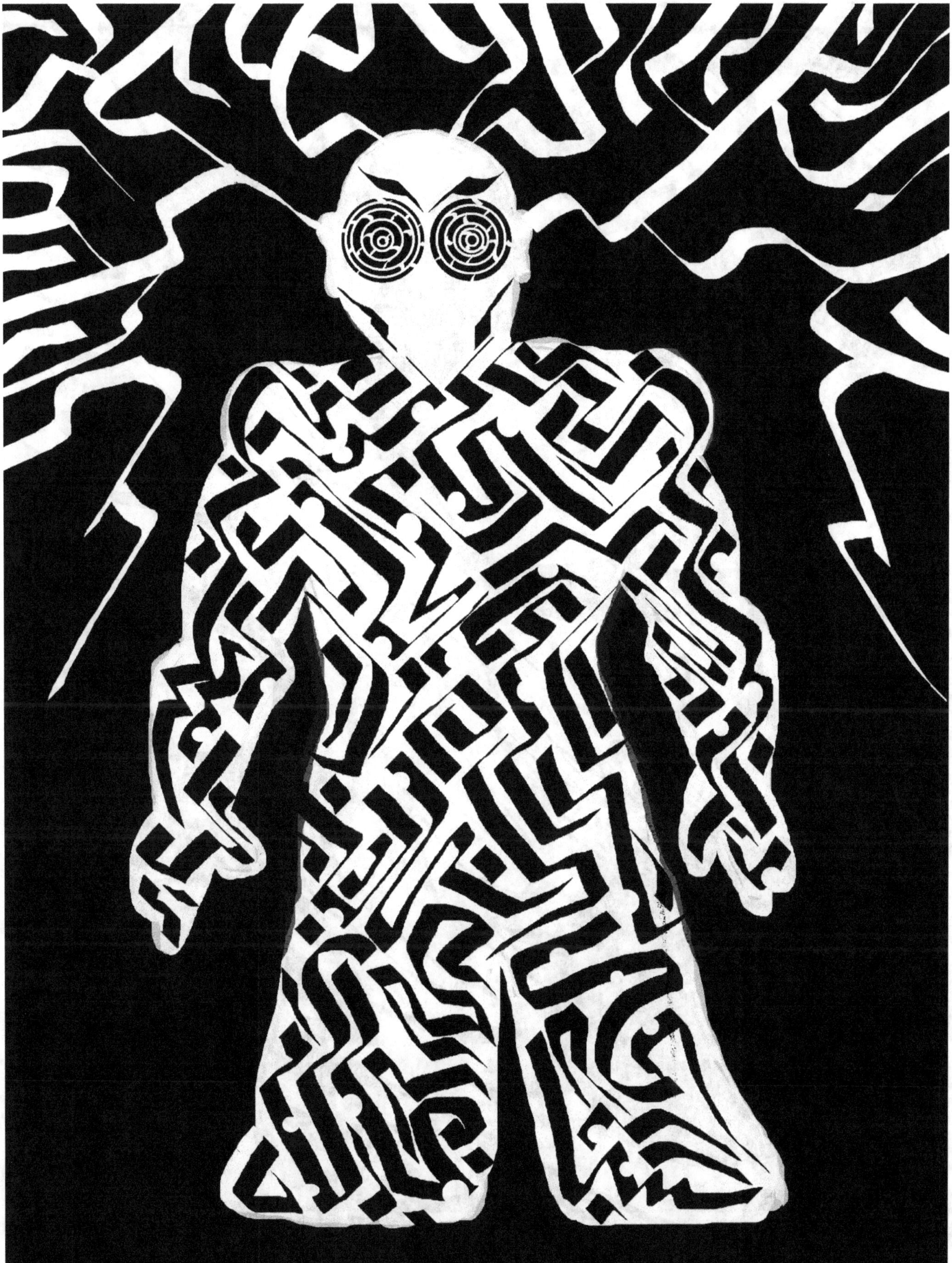

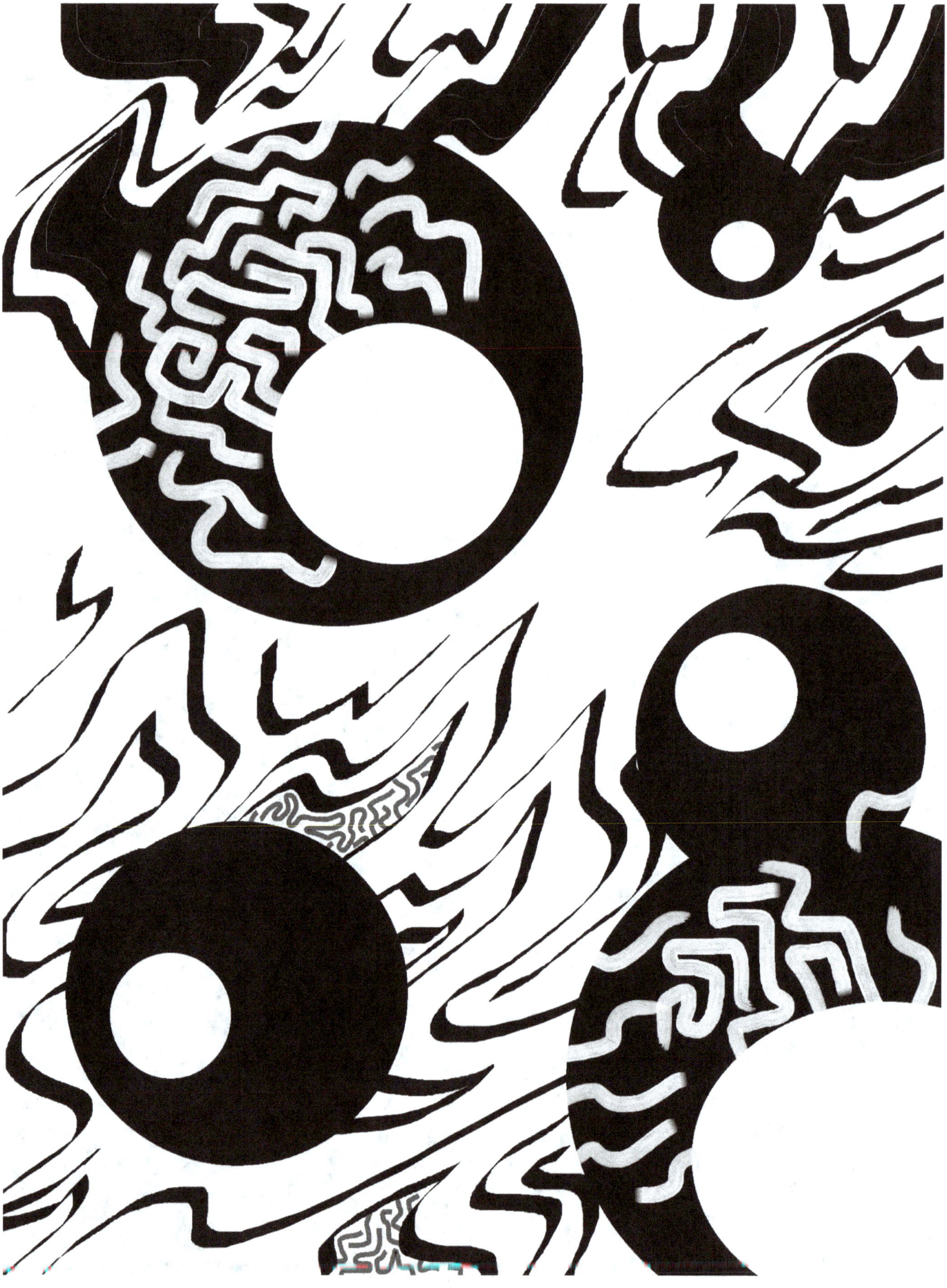

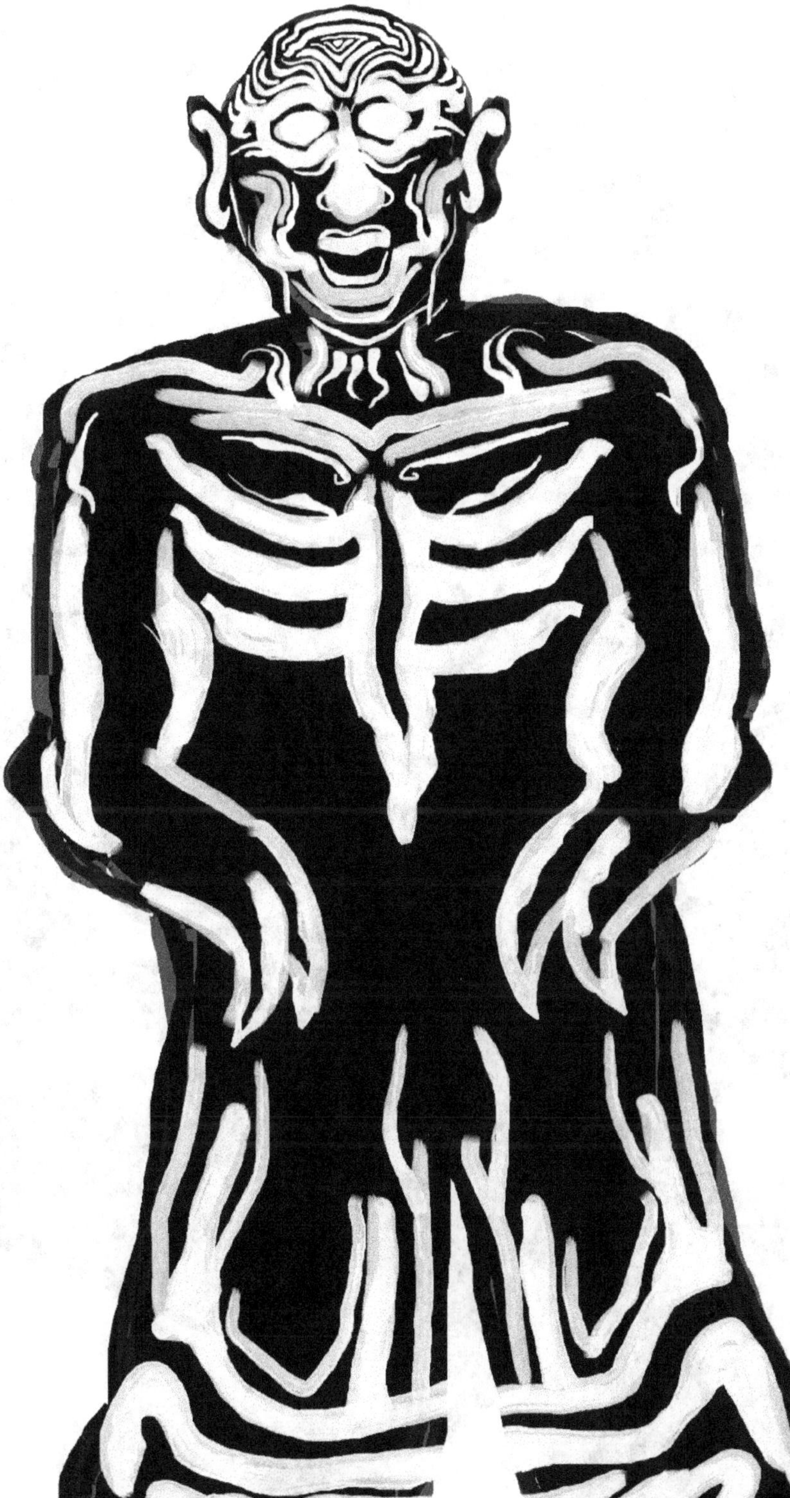

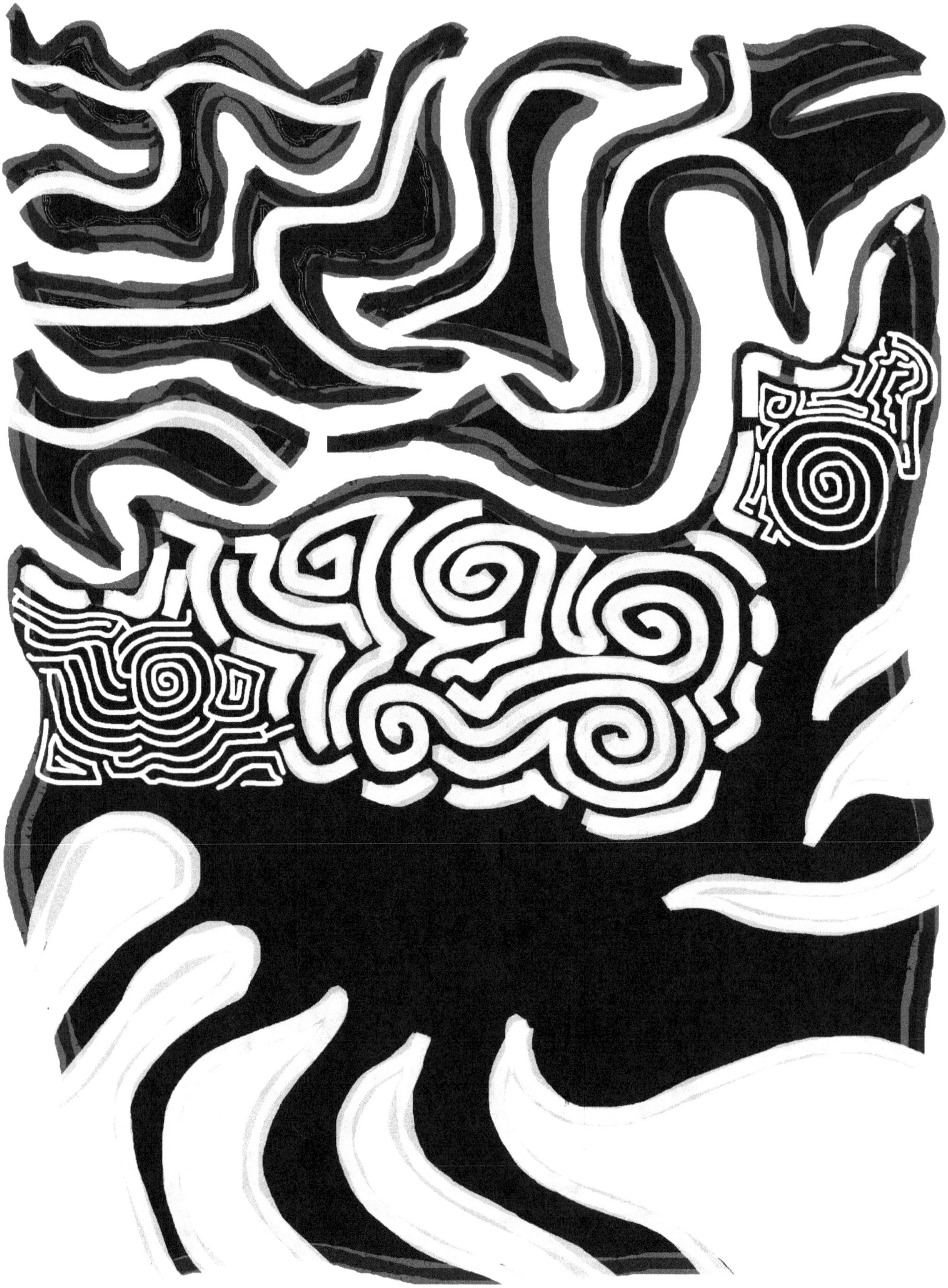

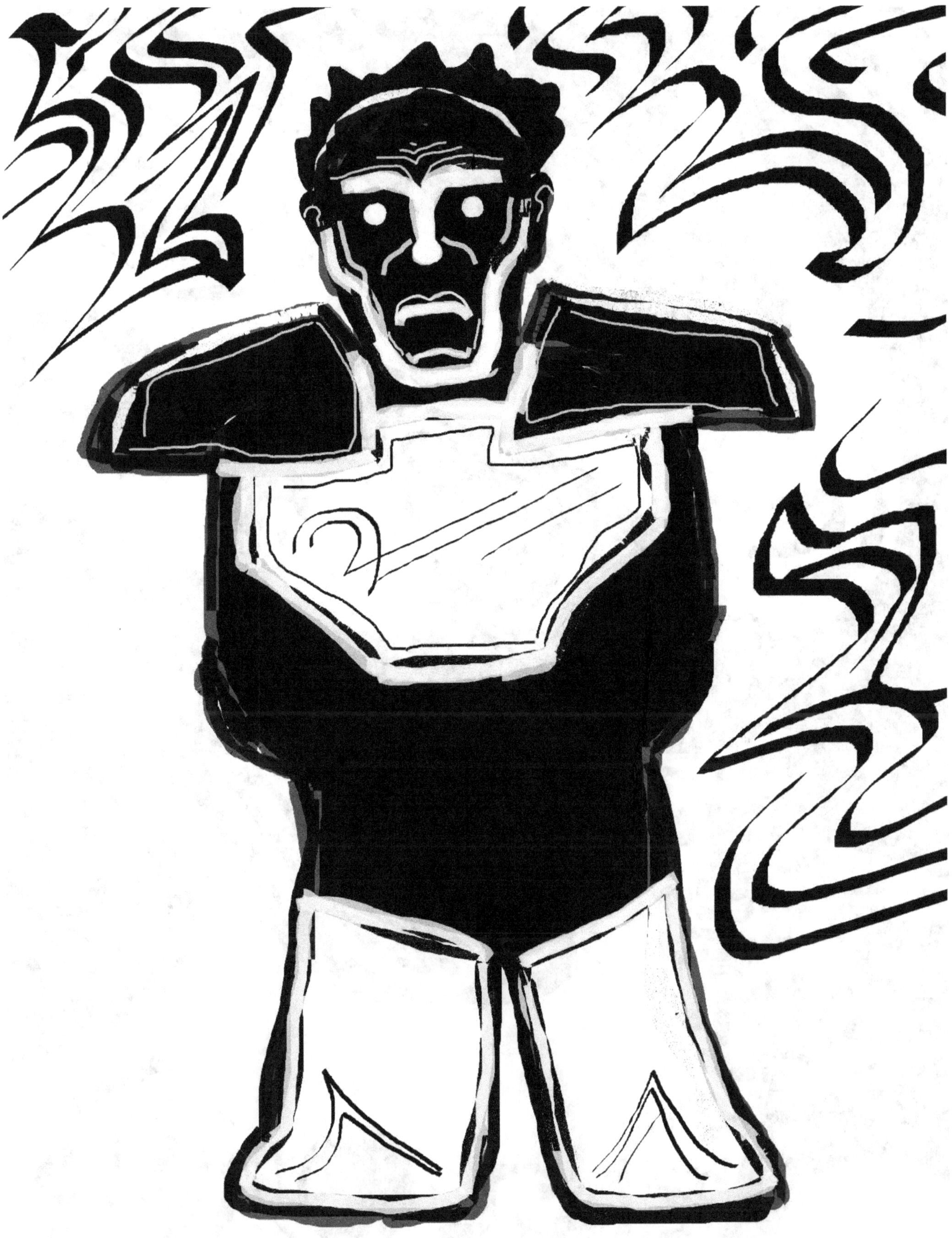

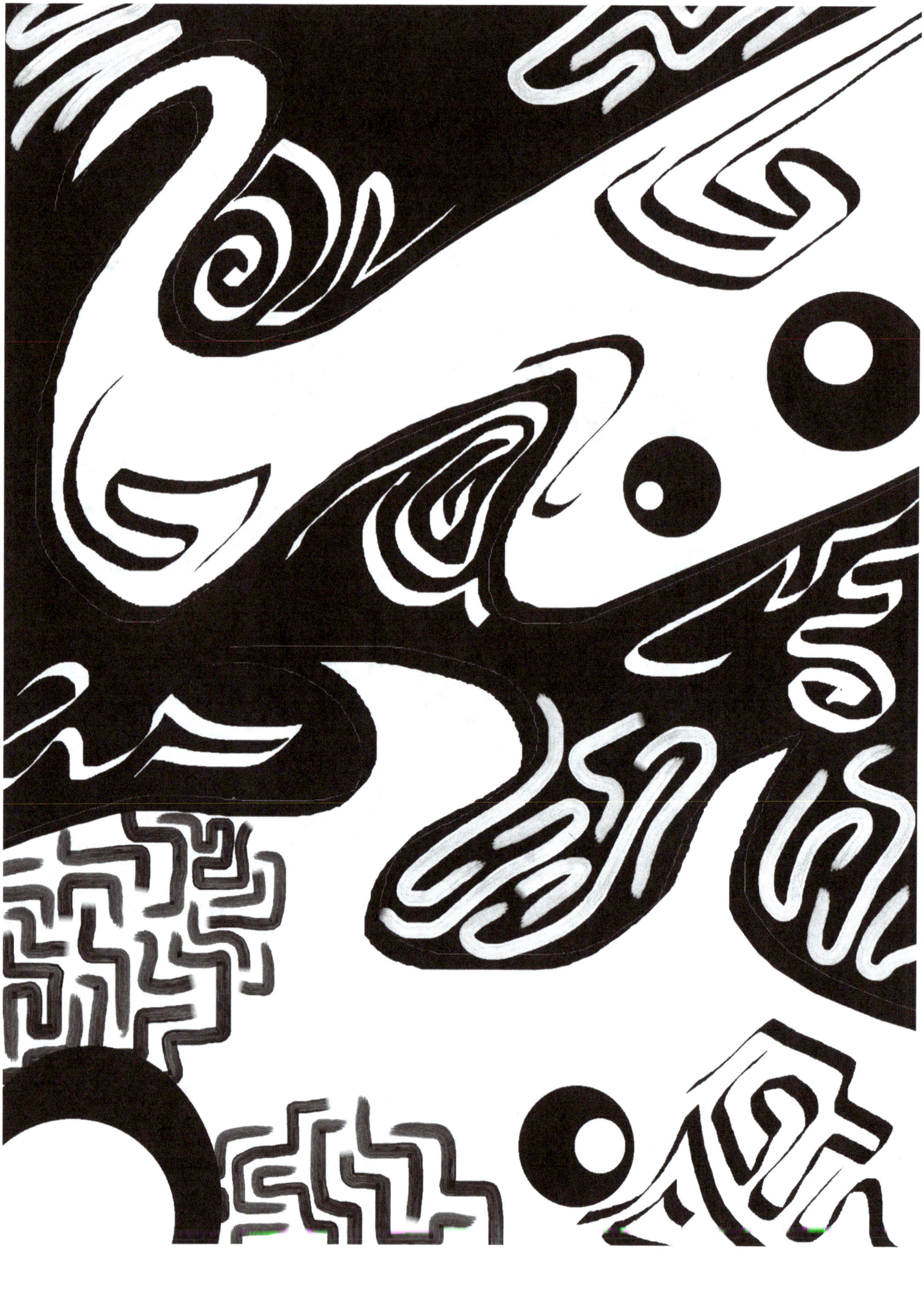

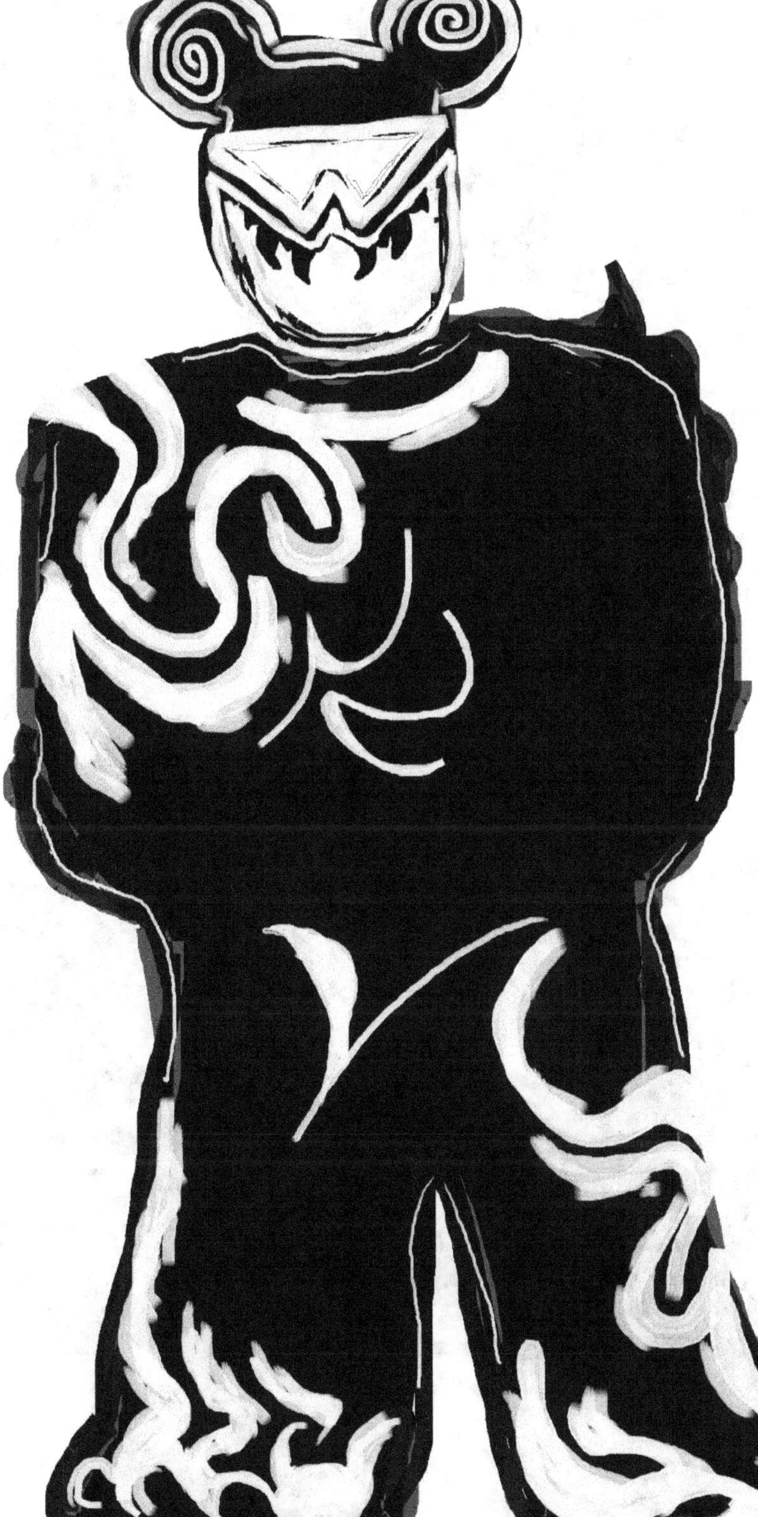

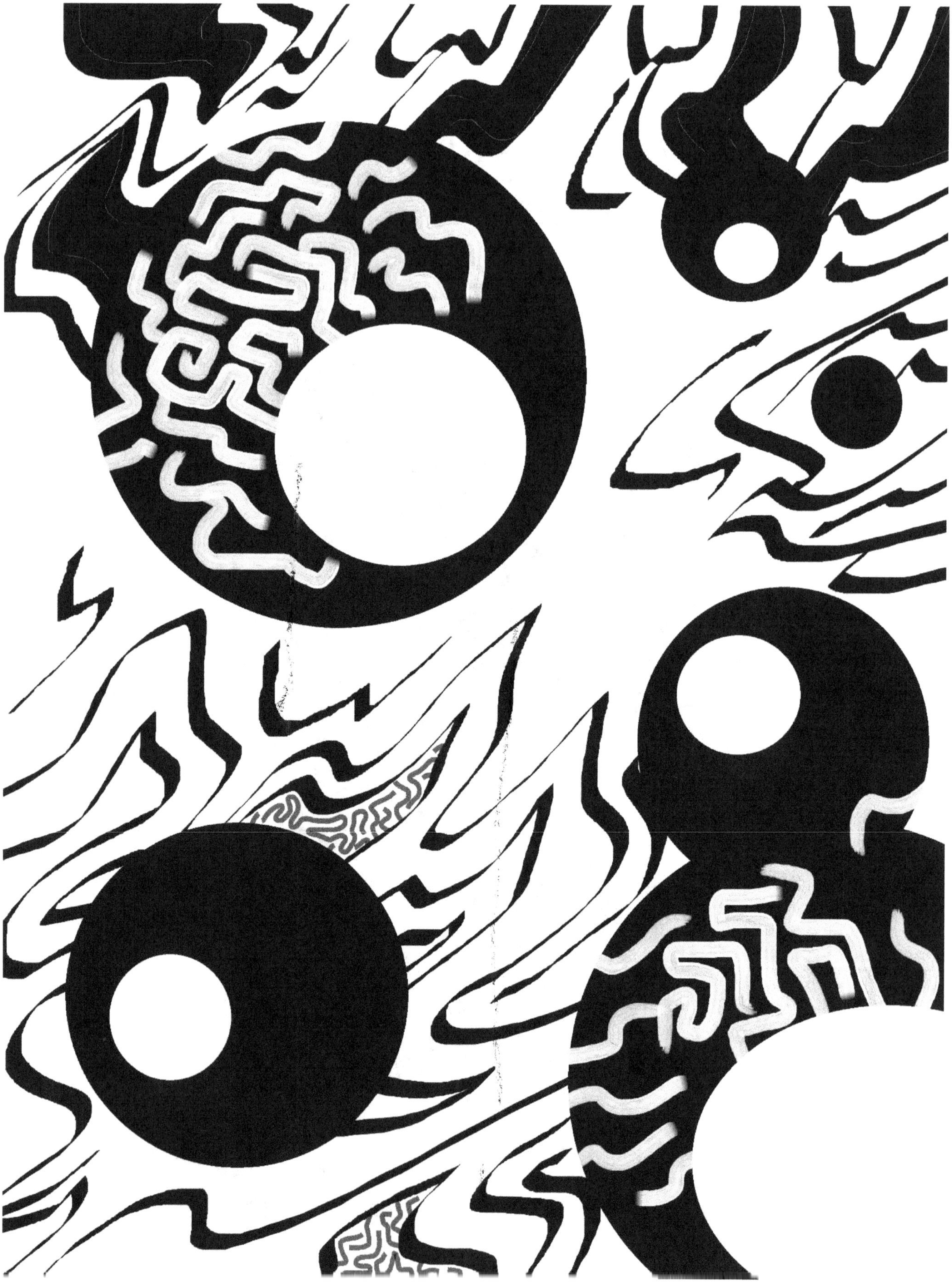

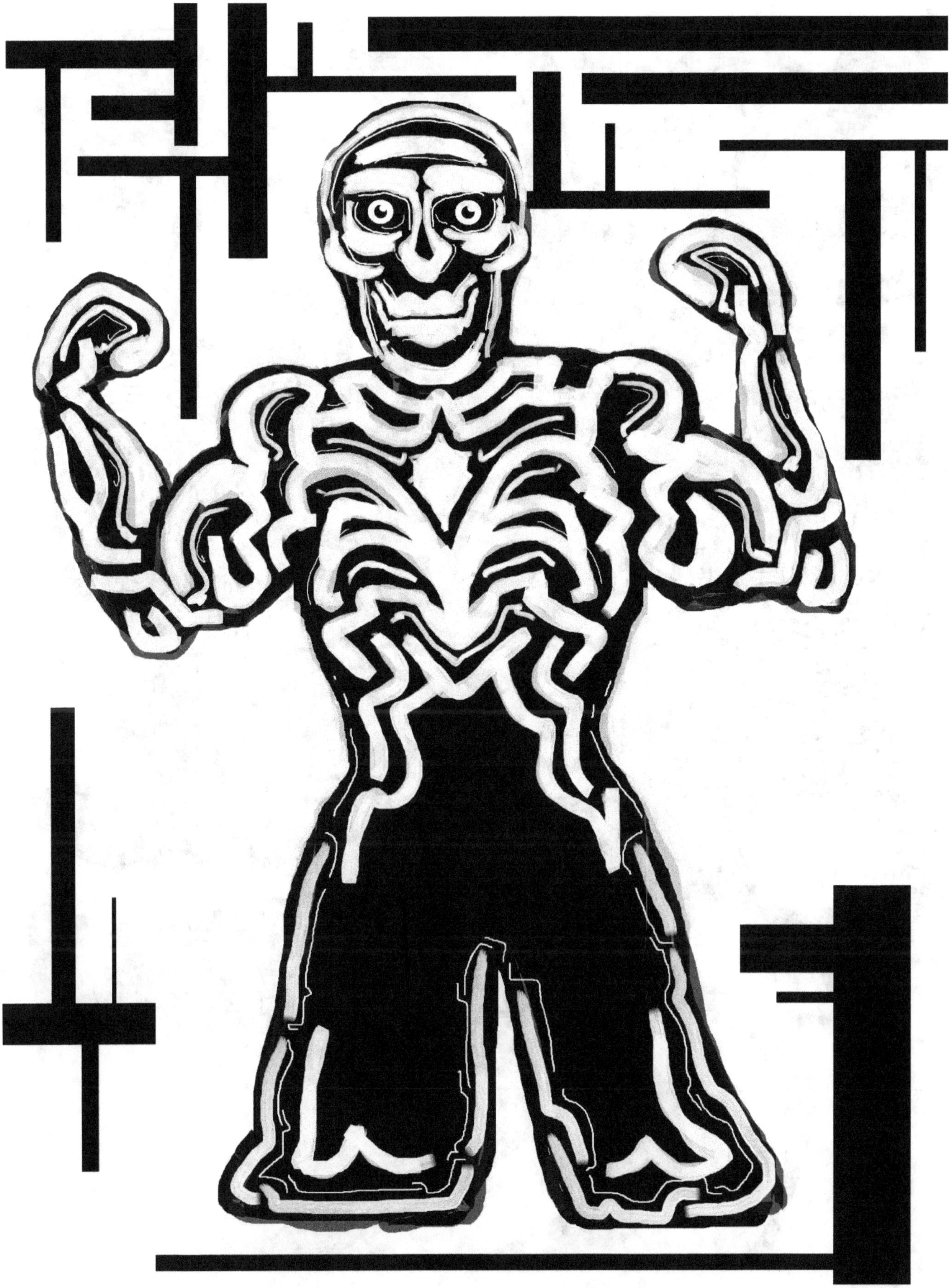

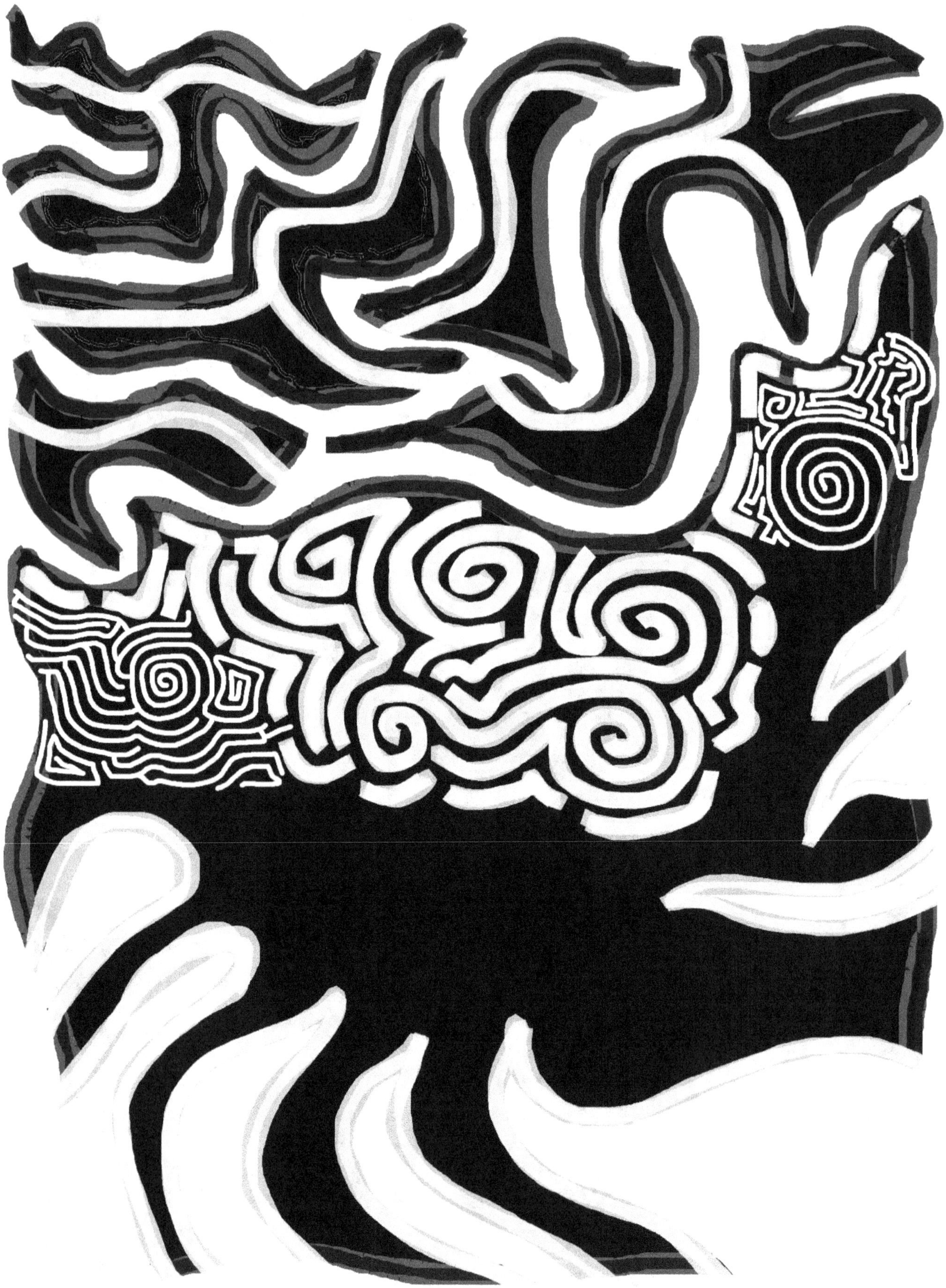

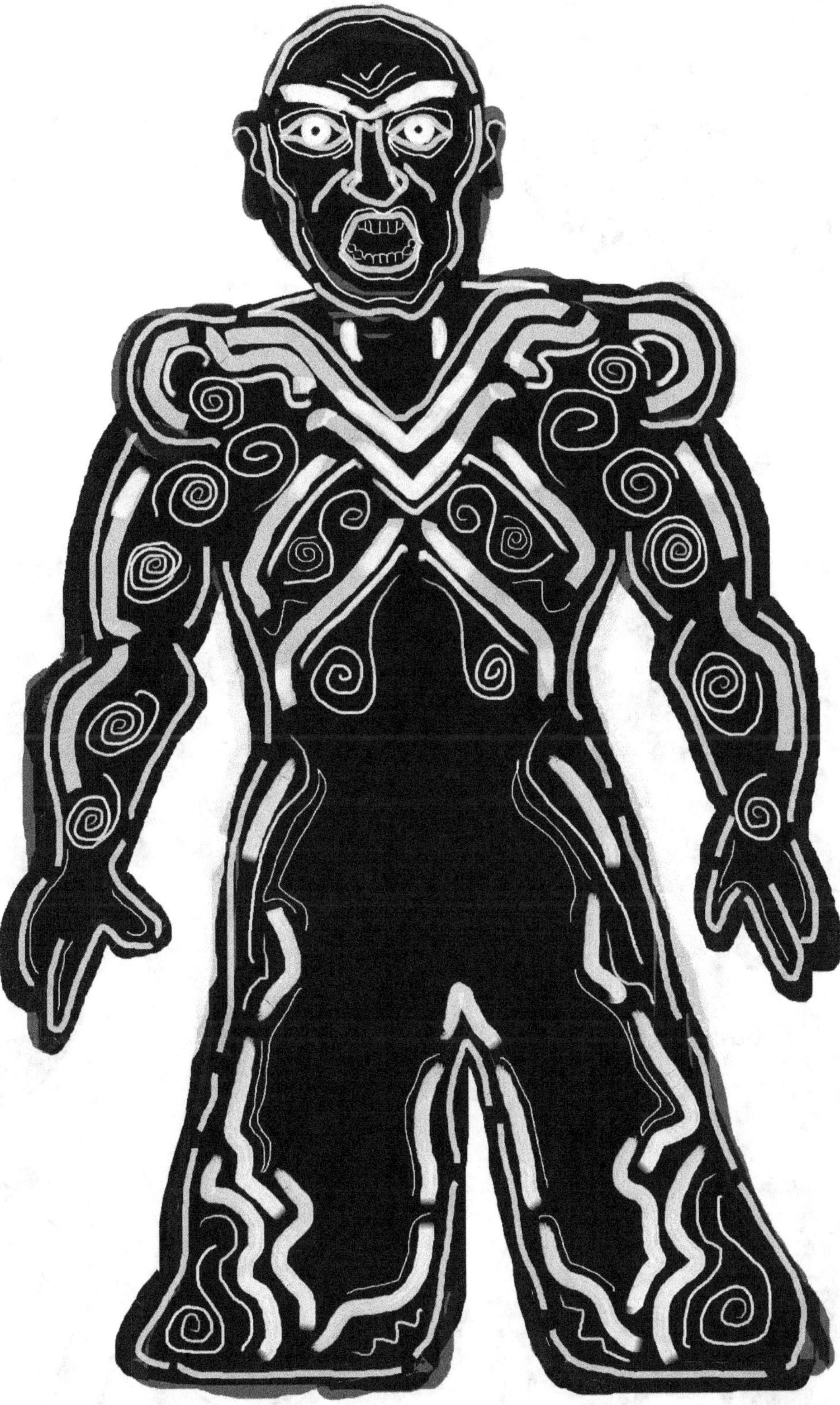

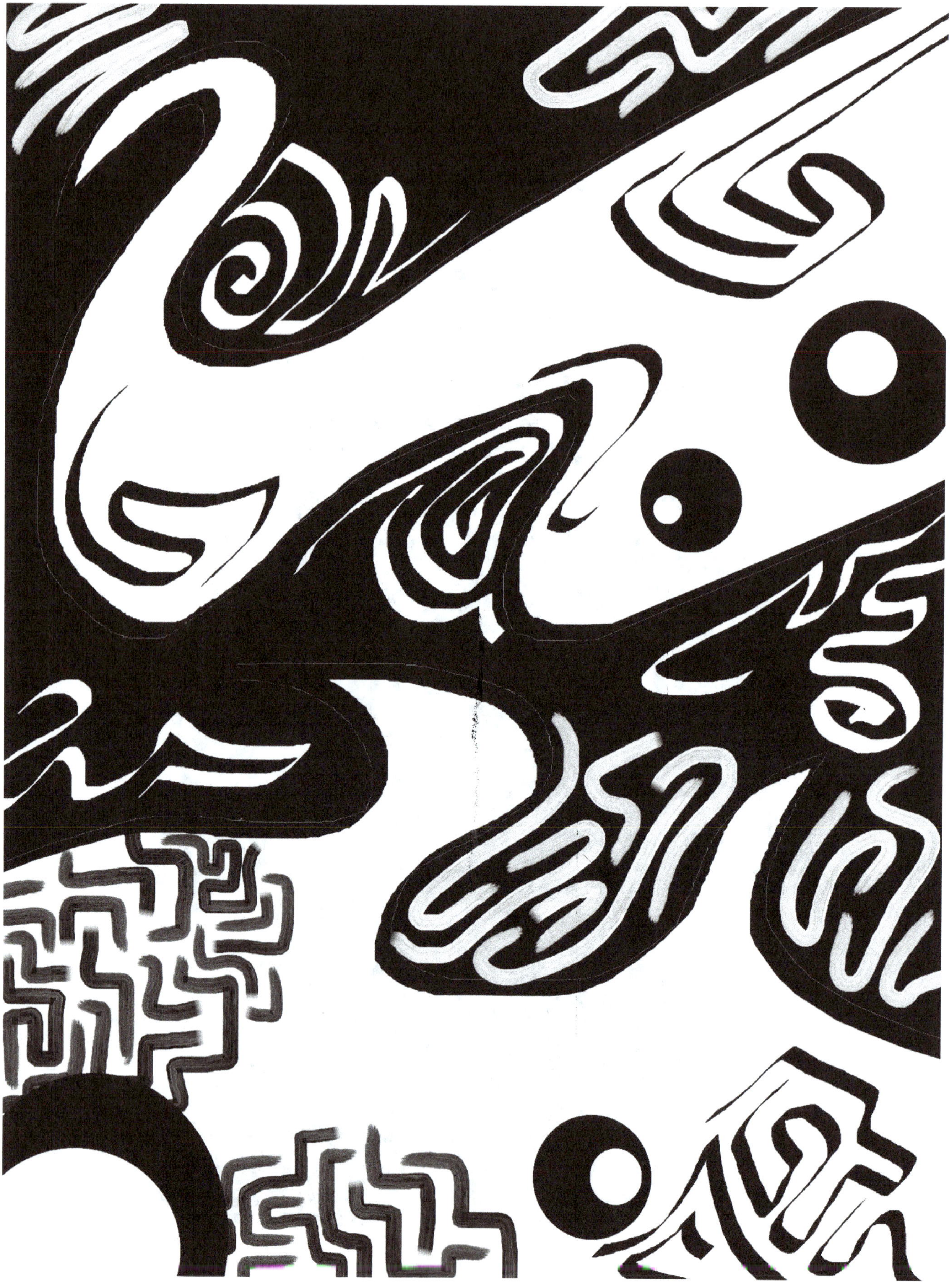

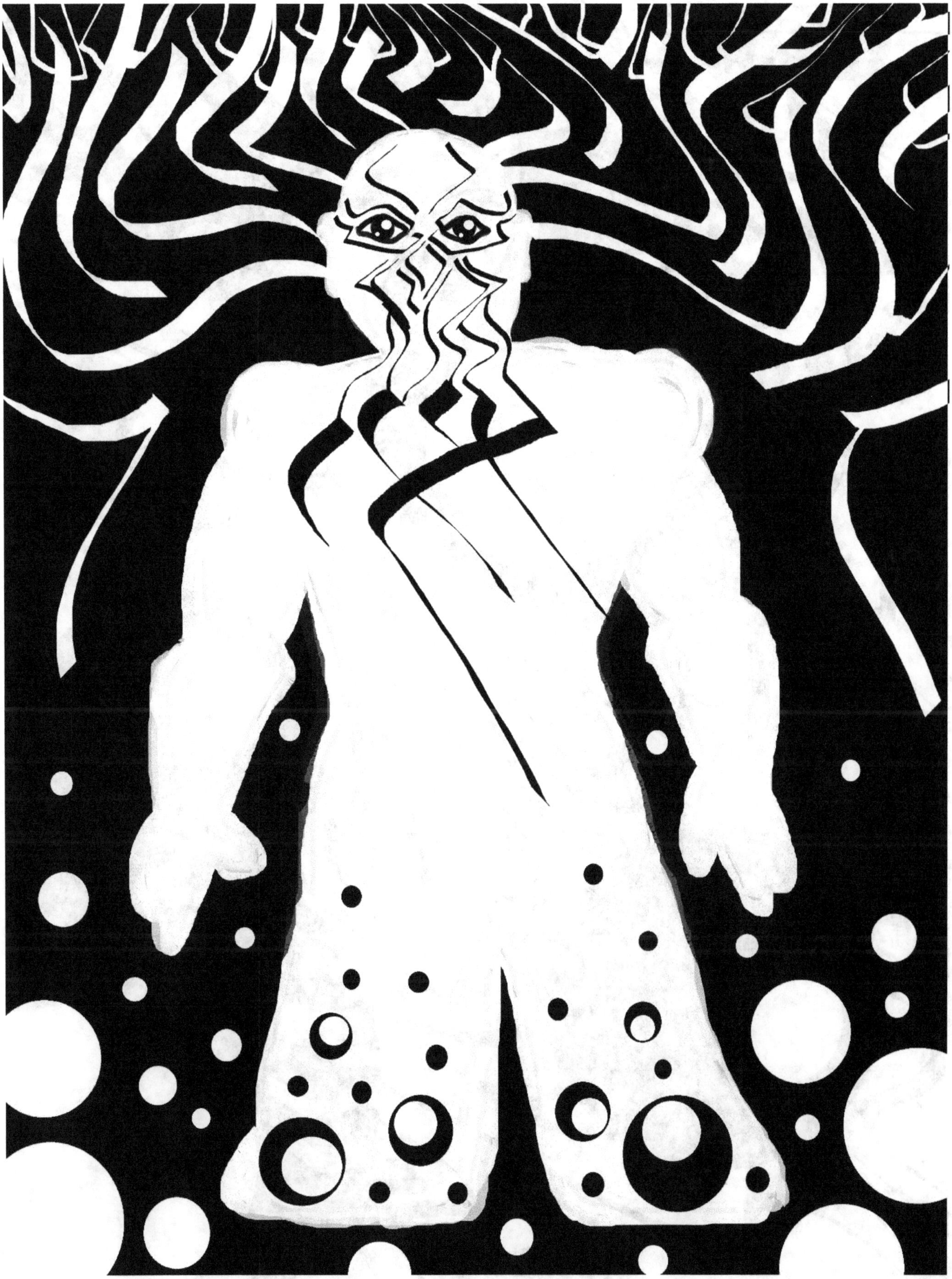

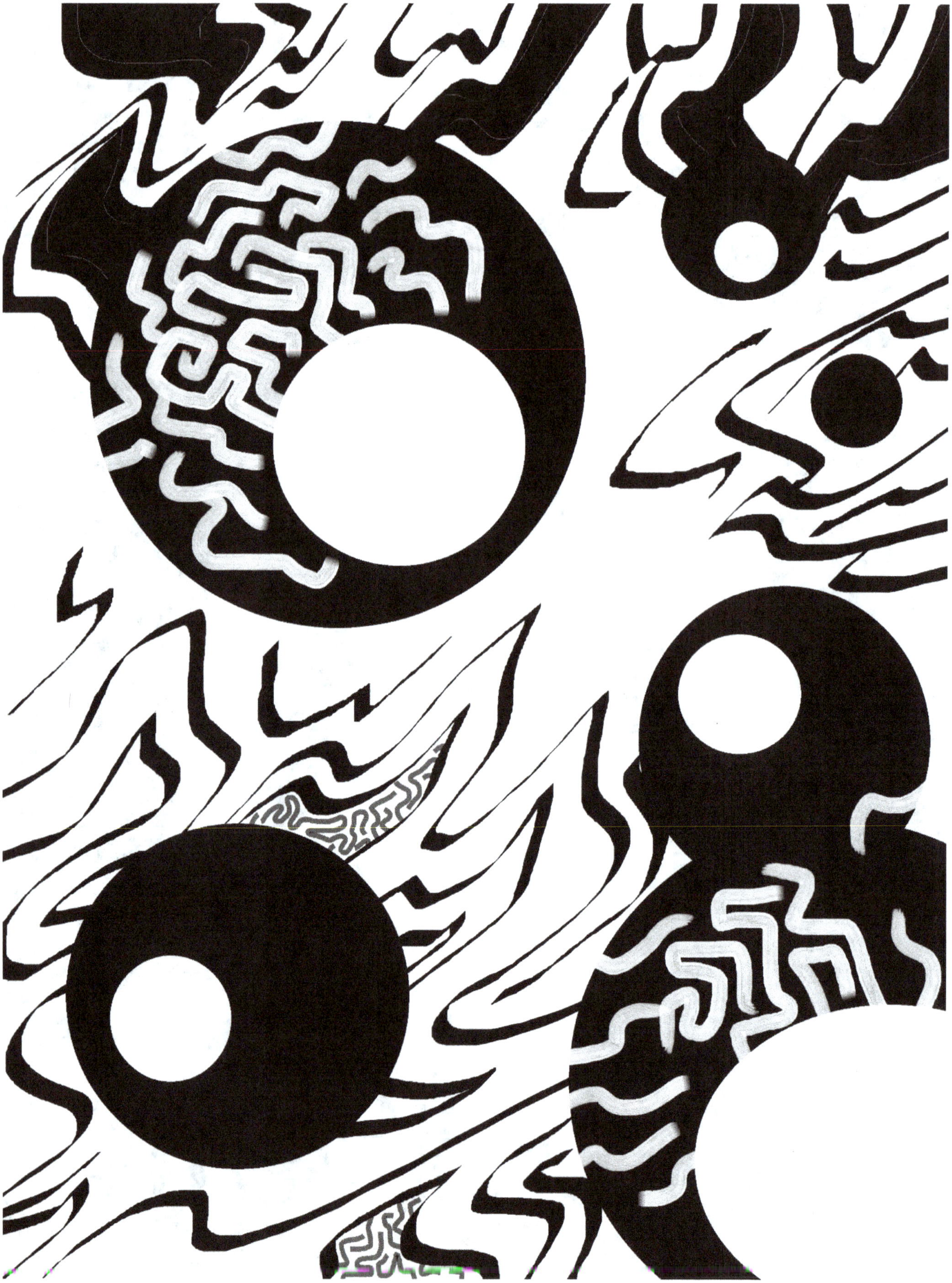

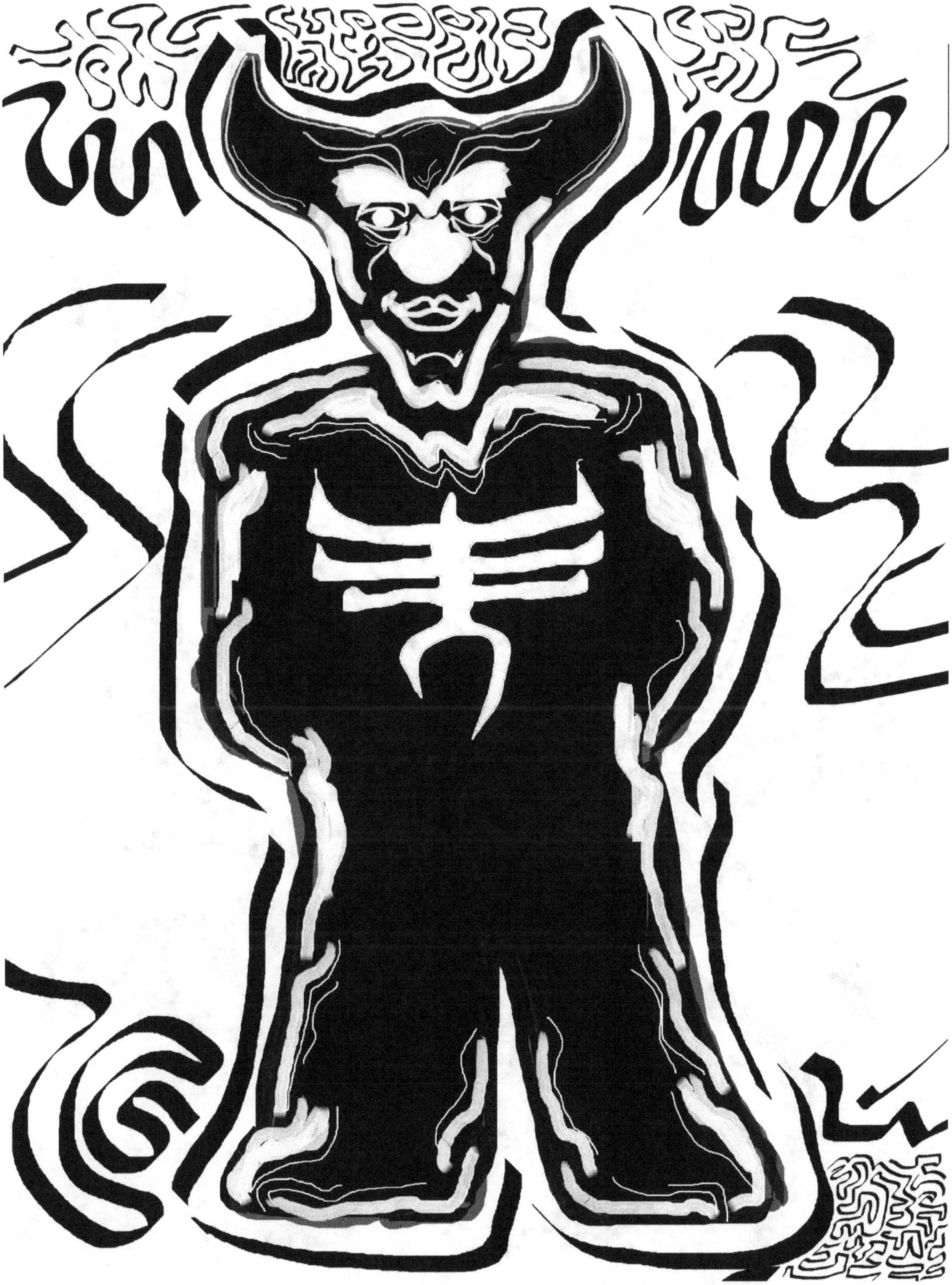

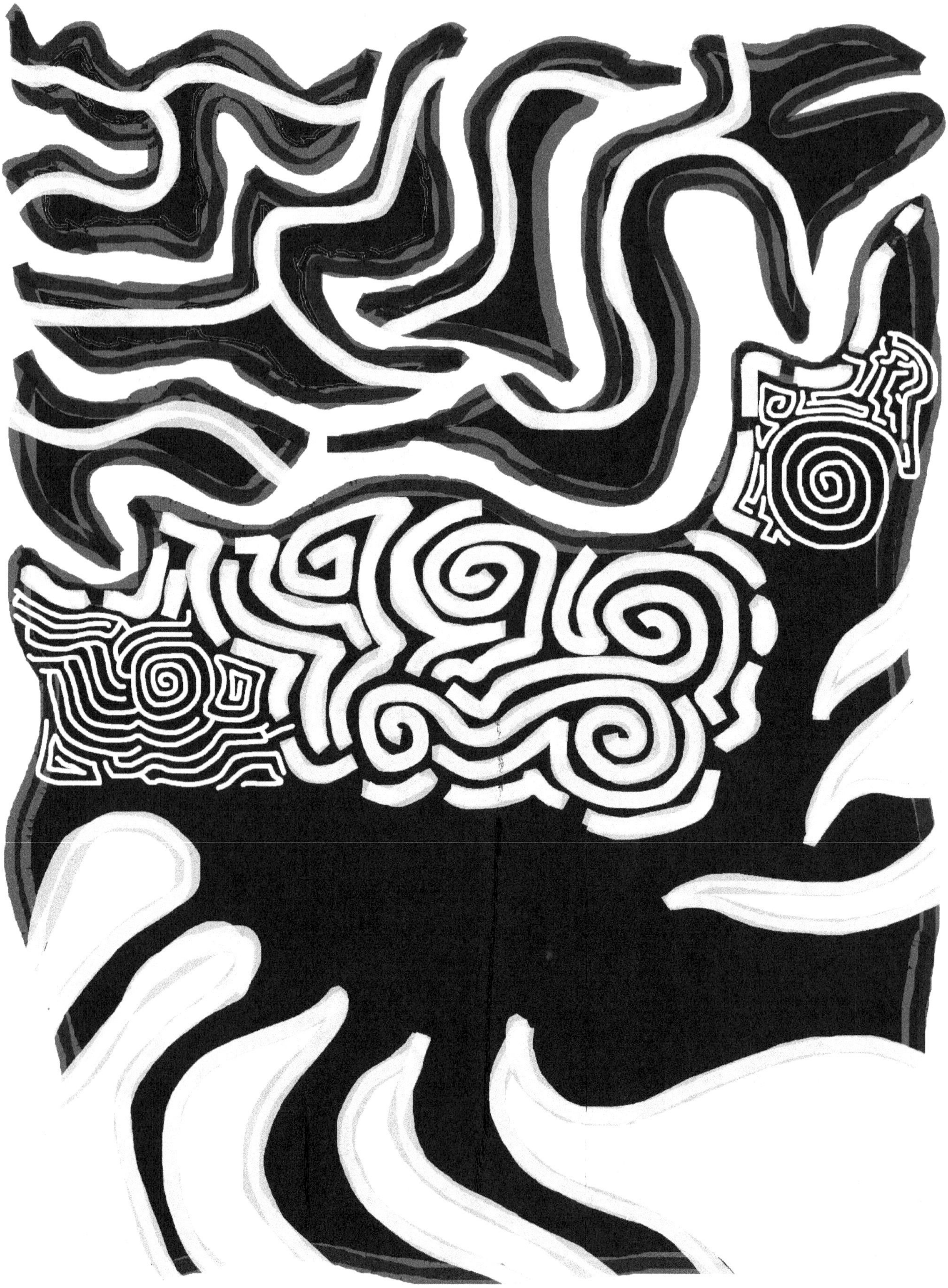

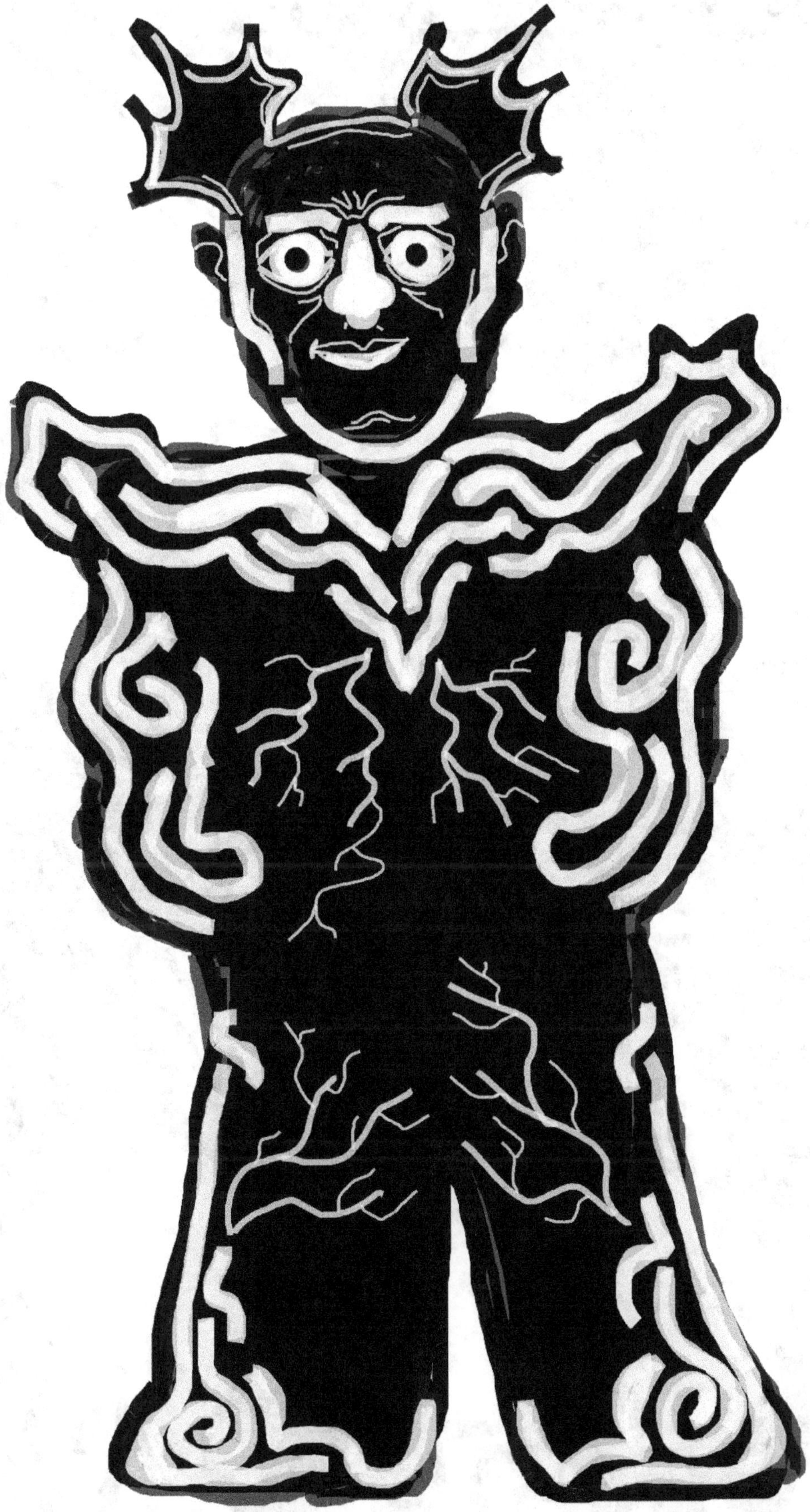

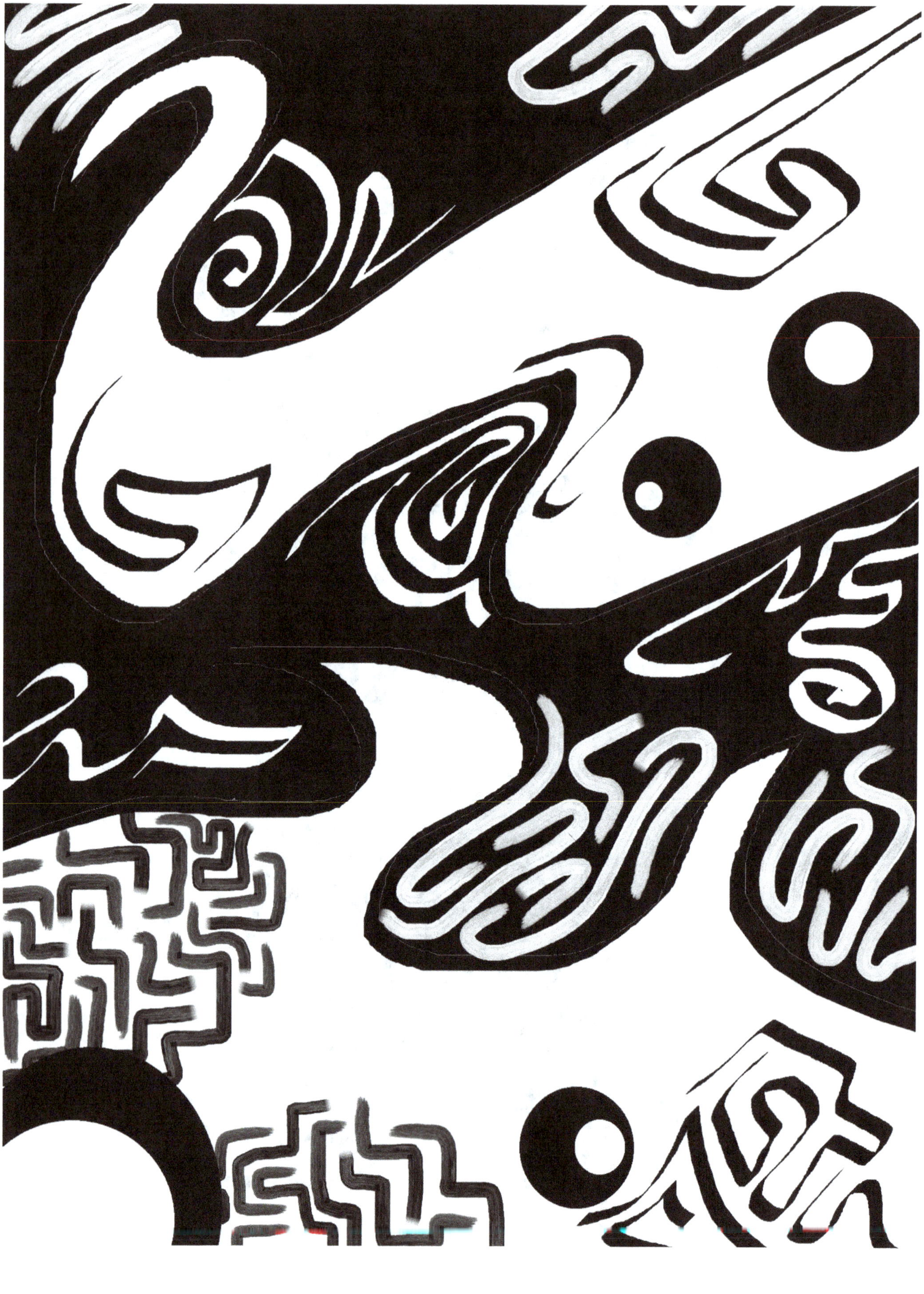

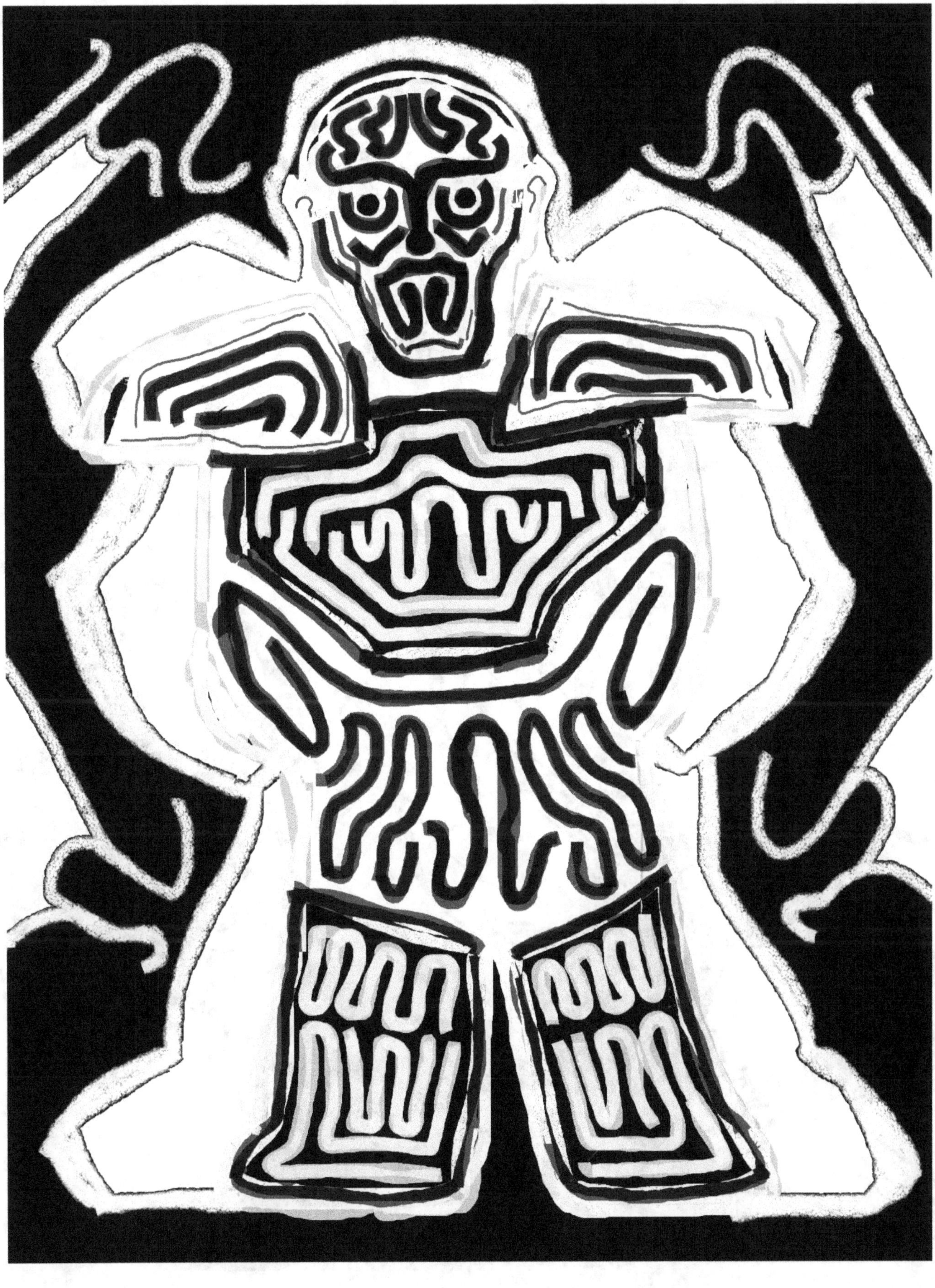

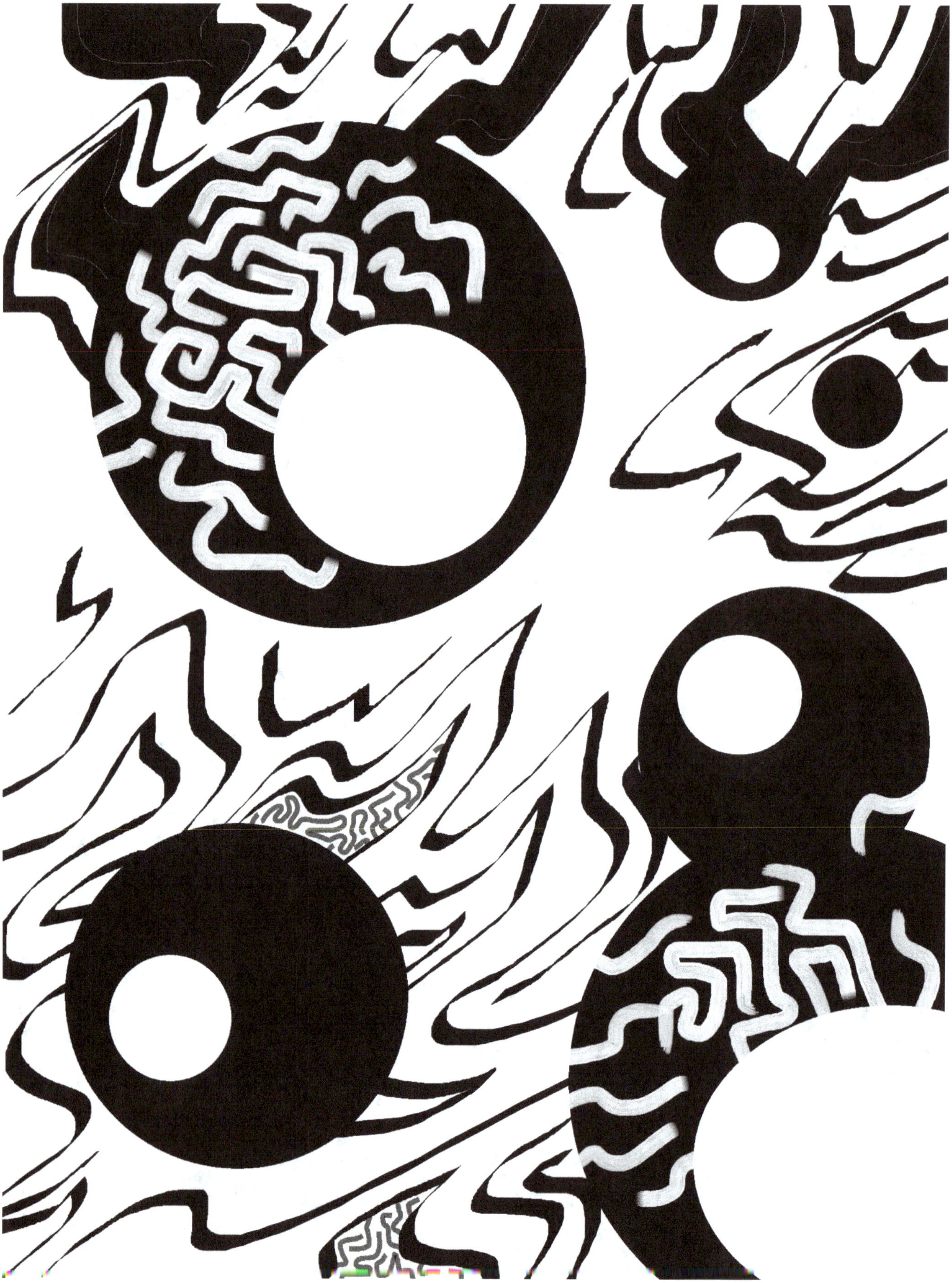

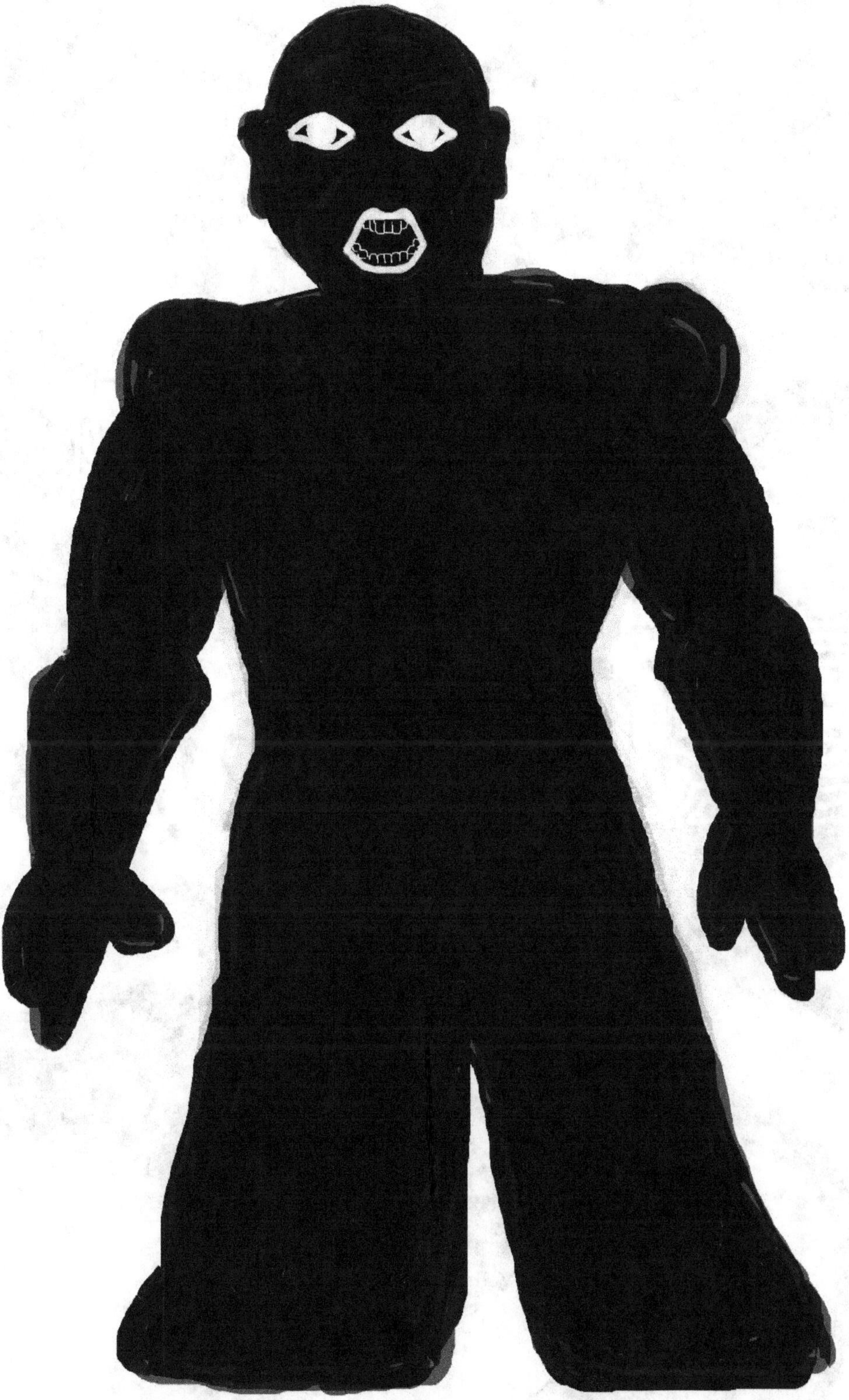

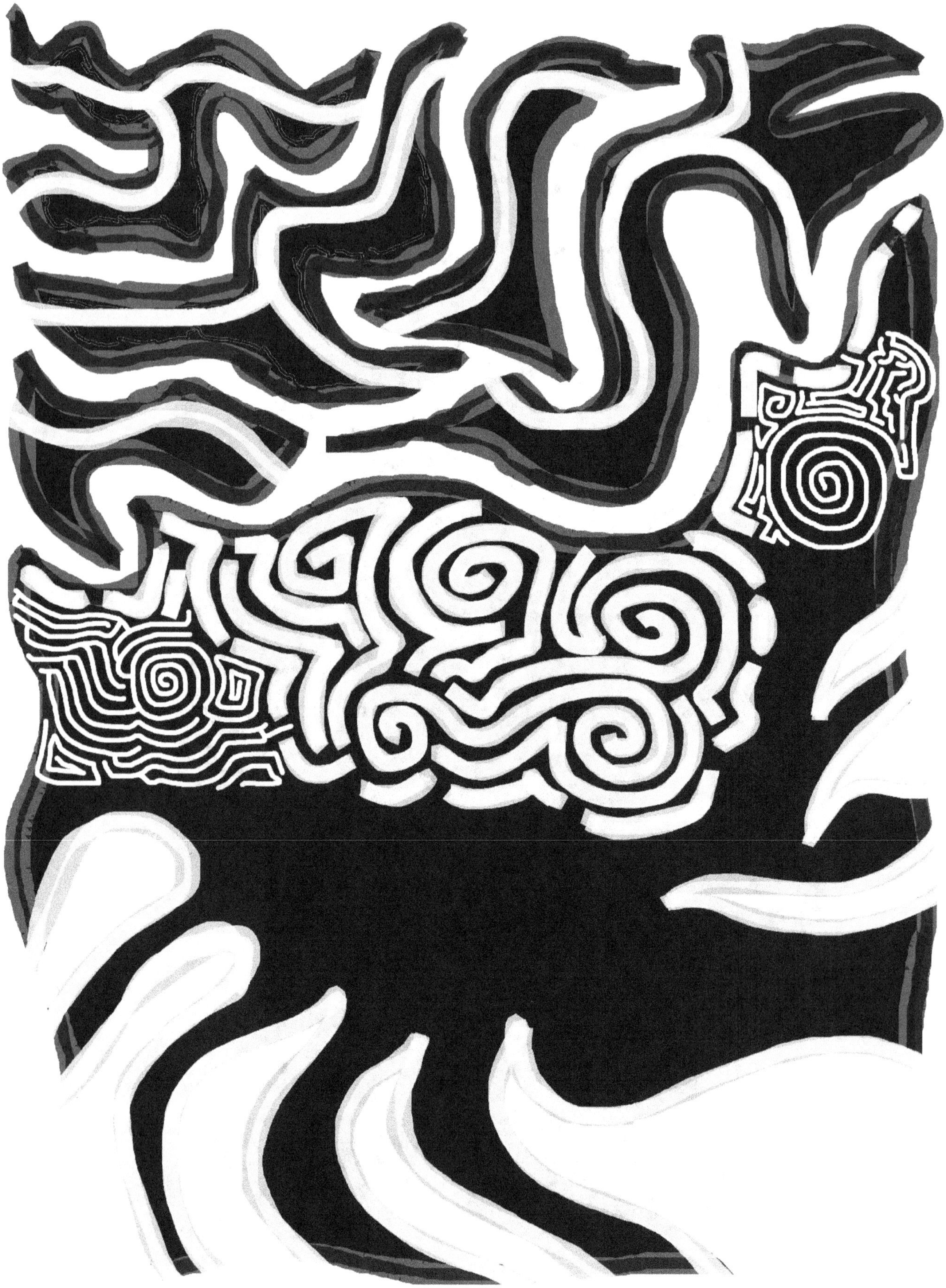

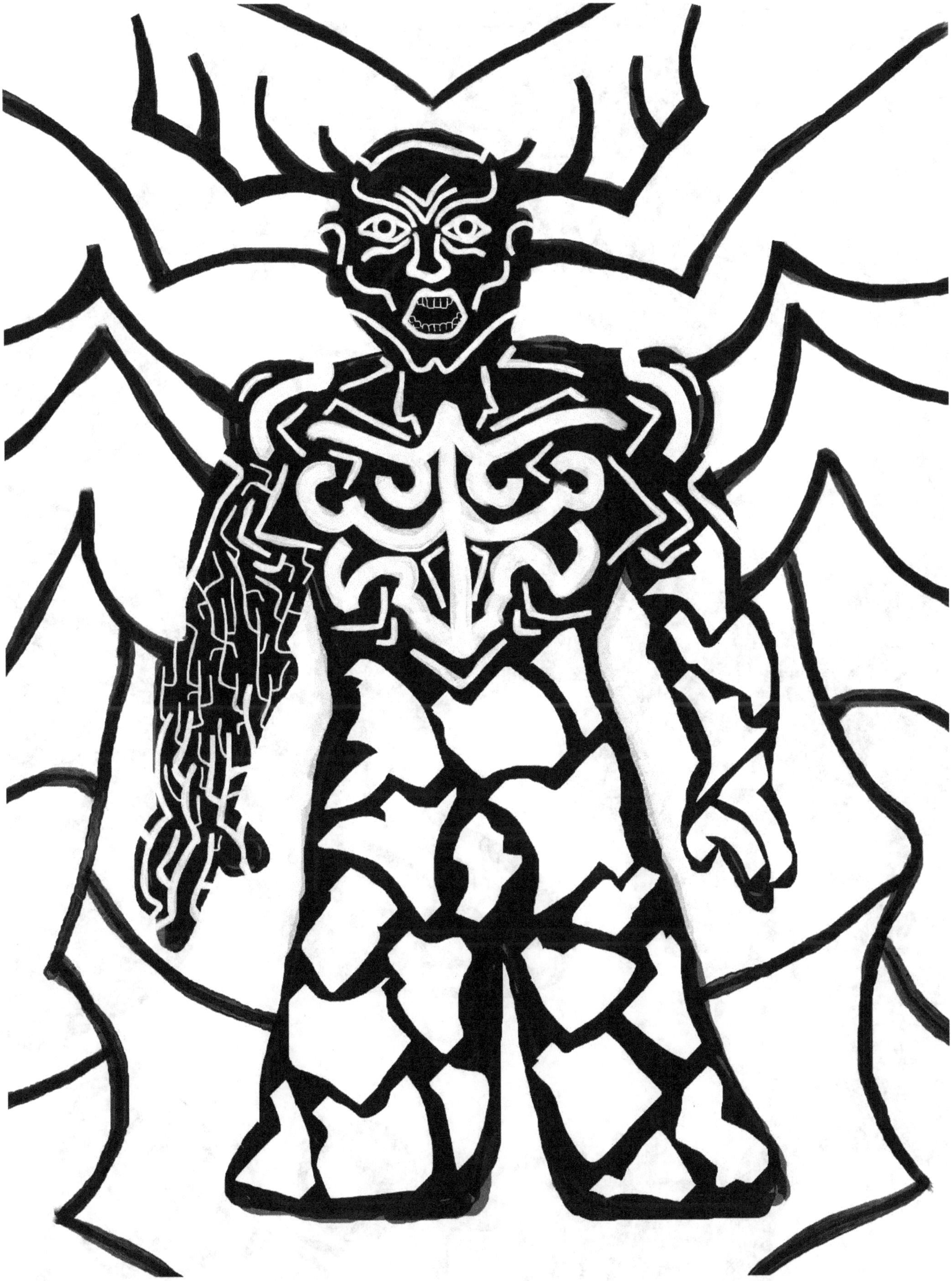

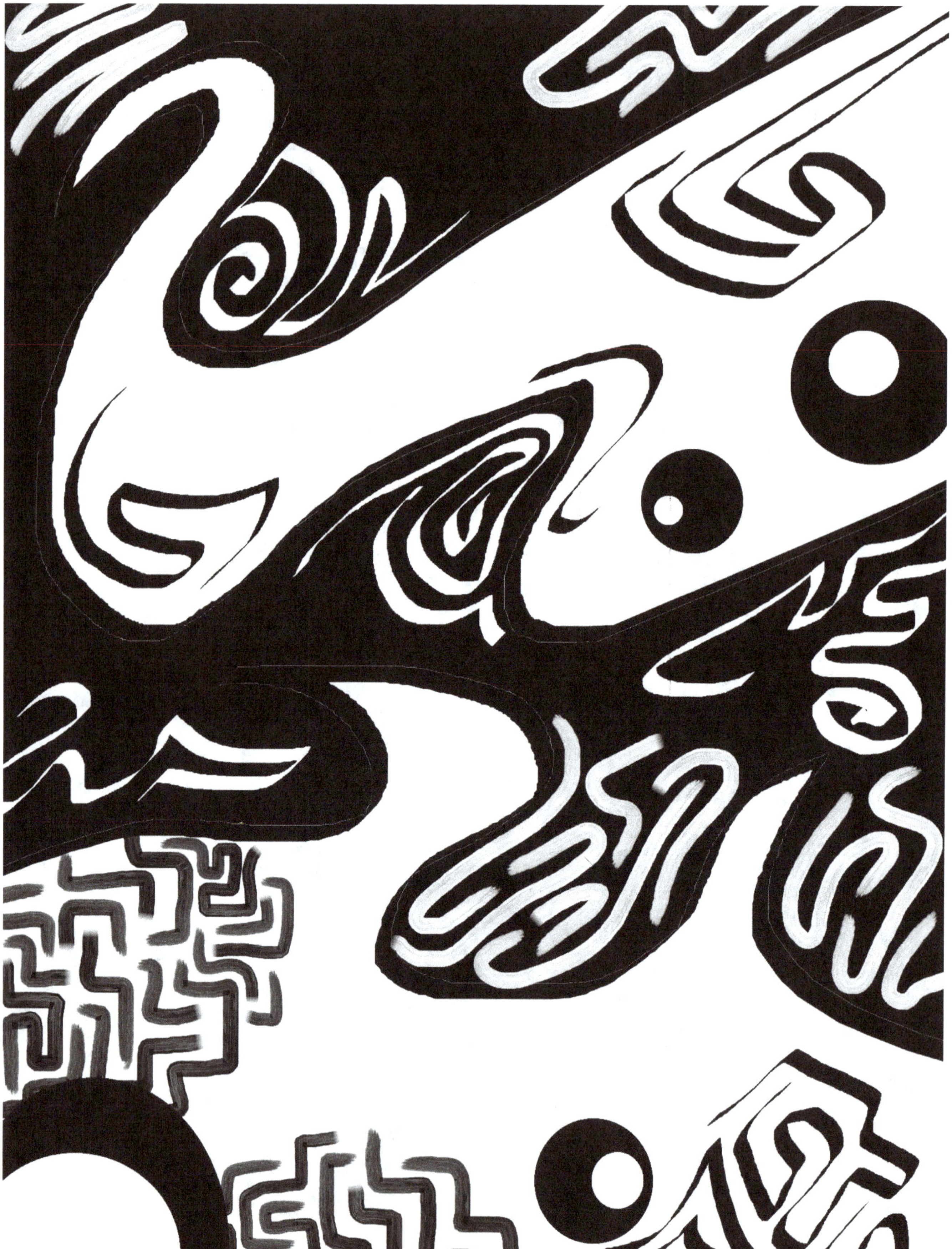

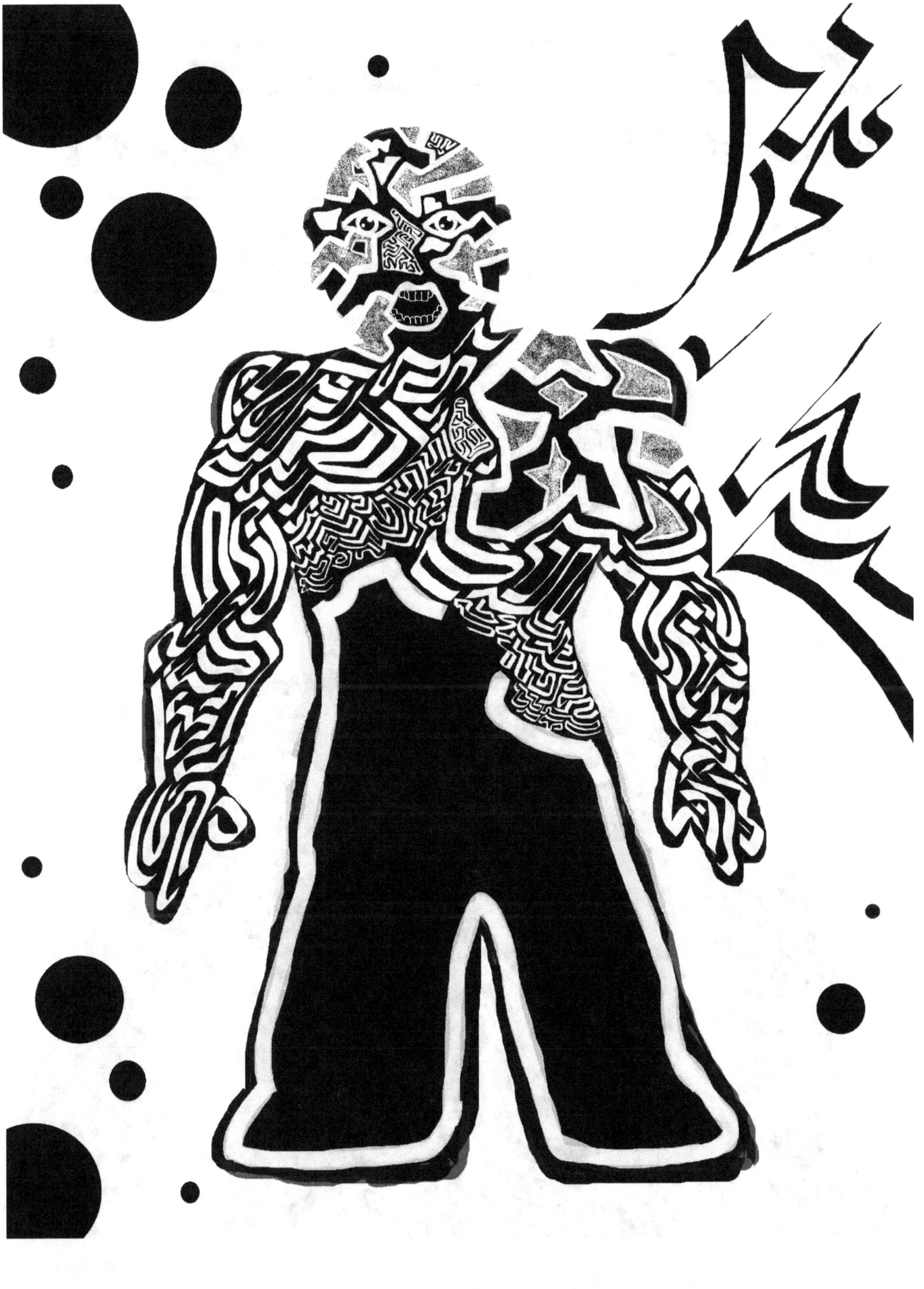

JAVELINA
ROAM THE NIGHT

COLORING BOOK

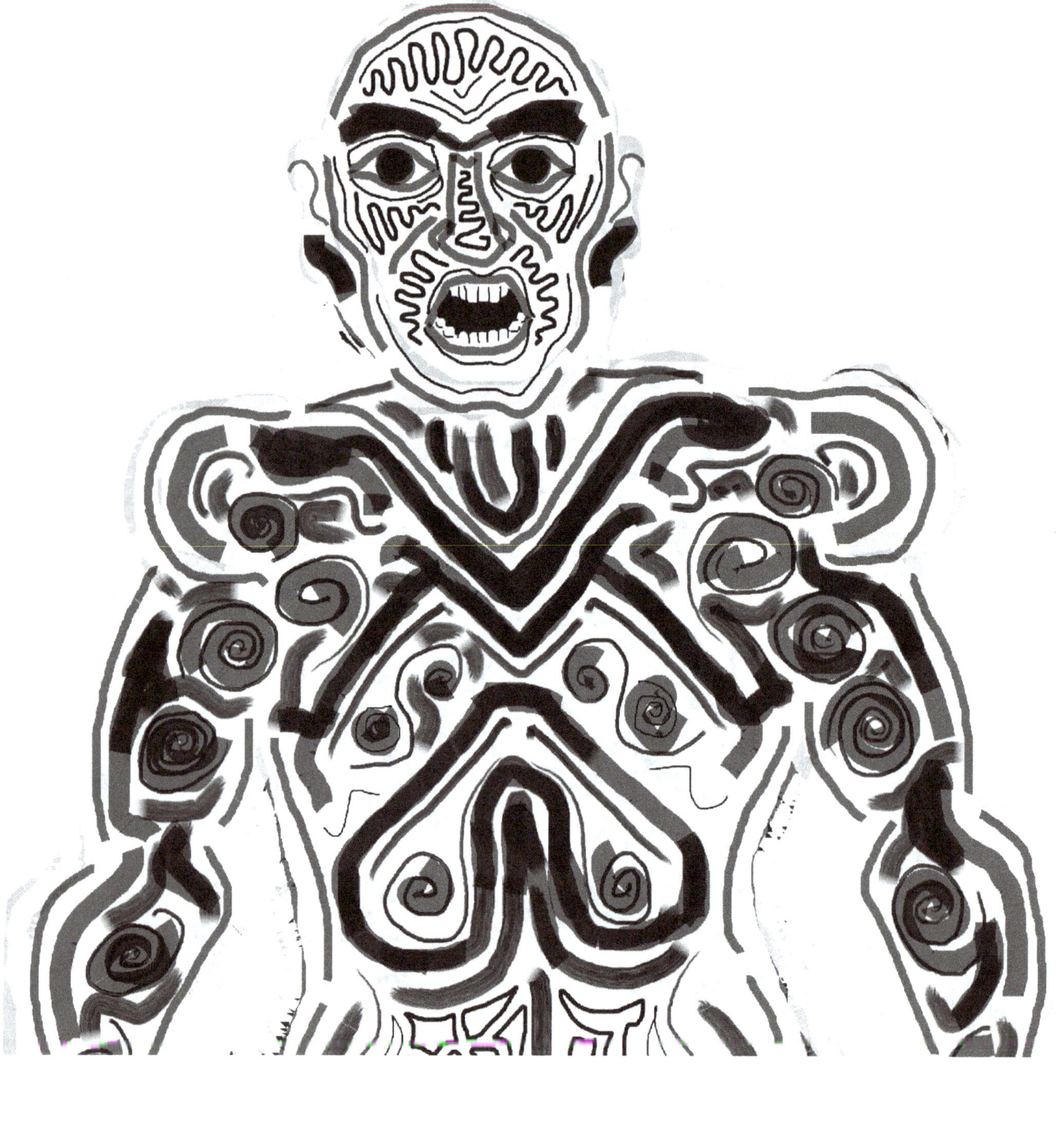

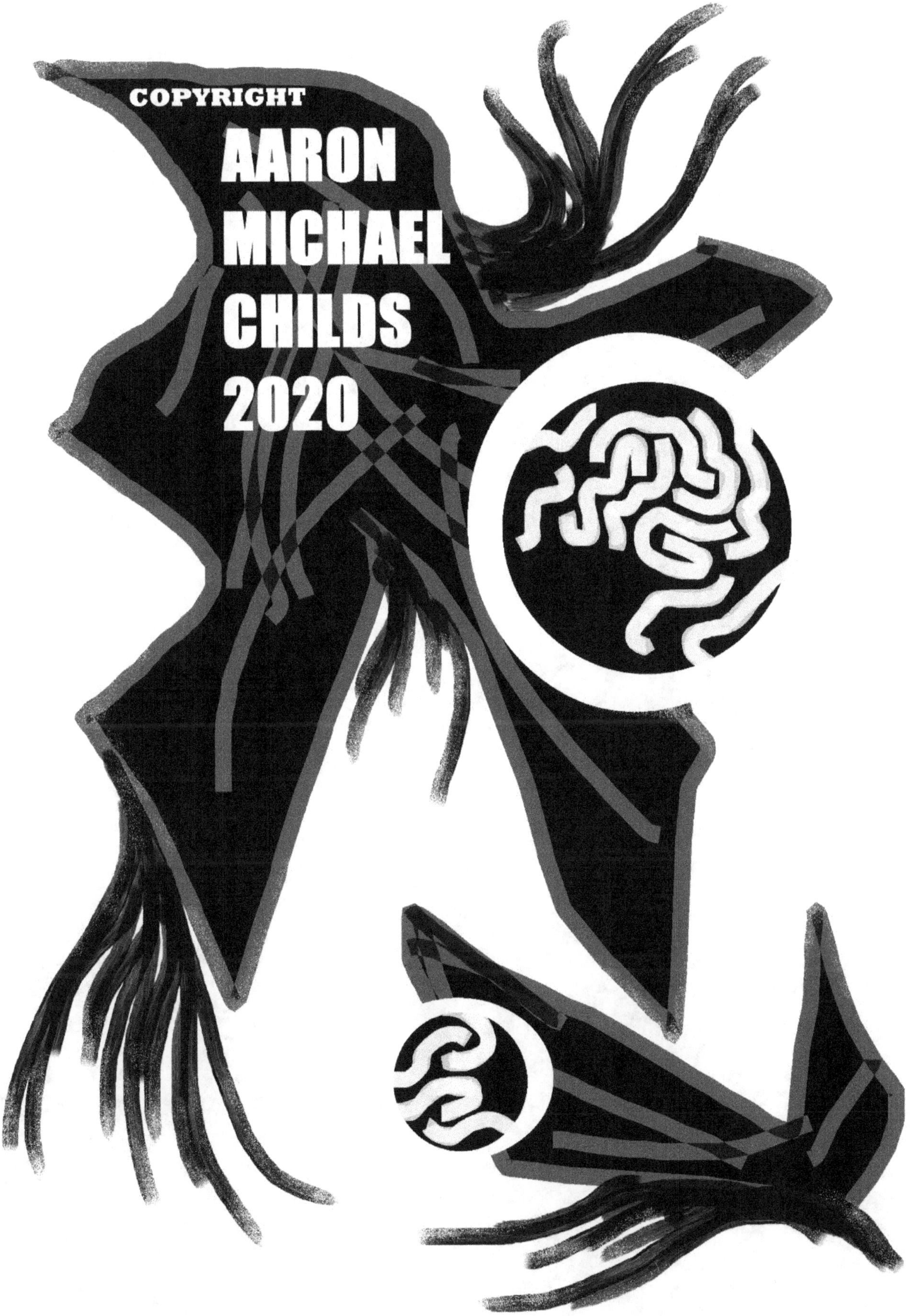
COPYRIGHT
AARON
MICHAEL
CHILDS
2020

www.ingramcontent.com/pod-product-compliance
Lightning Source LLC
Chambersburg PA
CBHW080515220526
45465CB00006B/2492
9798665856131